GOOD HOUSEKEEPING

MICROWAVE
COOKERY
COURSE

GOOD HOUSEKEEPING

MICROWAVE
COOKERY
COURSE

MARIE EMMERSON

EBURY PRESS
LONDON

Published by **E**bury **P**ress
Division of the **N**ational **M**agazine **C**ompany **L**td
Colquhoun **H**ouse
27–37 **B**roadwick **S**treet
London W1V 1FR

First impression 1986

ISBN 0 85223 596 8 (hardback)
   0 85223 446 5 (paperback)

Edited by **L**aurine **C**roasdale

Designed by **B**ob **H**ook and **I**vor **C**laydon
Illustrations by **R**aymond **B**urrows
Photography by **J**ohn **H**eseltine
Styling by **A**ndrea **L**ampton

Filmset by Advanced Filmsetters (Glasgow) Ltd.
Printed and bound in Great Britain by
Butler & Tanner Ltd, Frome

CONTENTS

INTRODUCTION

The microwave cooker and its extraordinary powers make it seem like a miracle box, and all sorts of exaggerated claims have been made about it. The advantages of microwave cooking, however, are many. The microwave cooker is extremely fast for thawing and cooking; it takes up very little space and can be housed on a work surface and plugged in to any 13 amp socket outlet; the cooker is always cool as all the microwave energy goes into the cooking and not into the room; it uses less fuel than other forms of cooking; food can be cooked in any type of non-metallic food container. If food is not covered and splashing occurs it is simply a matter of wiping the cooking cavity with a damp cloth, thus cleaning is easy. The biggest appeal of the microwave cooker is the speed and variety of cooking operations which can be carried out. Food can be thawed, cooked or reheated in a fraction of the time taken using conventional methods.

Any new appliance takes time to get used to, and the microwave cooker is no different. In some ways, it is unfortunate that the appliance is so versatile, because at the initial stages it is difficult for a new user to establish exactly what to do to get experience without wasting ingredients.

This microwave cookery course is intended to help both the novice and the experienced microwave owner. Each recipe is graded to be VERY EASY, EASY, or LESS EASY. For new users, the very easy recipes will give them the opportunity to get to know the controls and method of operation which in turn will give extra confidence when trying other recipes. For those with experience, the course includes plenty of scope for new and different recipes to add to their repertoire.

This book has maintained the usual sections, for example soups, starters, meat, poultry and fish: it can be used like any other cookery book but each section includes guidance about any special points concerning the type of food being cooked.

GENERAL INFORMATION ON MICROWAVE COOKERY

INSTALLATION

The microwave cooker can be plugged in virtually anywhere where it is convenient so long as it is positioned on a firm surface. However, it should not be placed on the top of other appliances, for example, a refrigerator, unless advice and confirmation have been sought from the cooker manufacturer. A number of models have been specifically designed to be built into kitchen units. However, should a microwave cooker be chosen which is not designed for this purpose, ask the manufacturer for specific information about the amount of space required for ventilation around the cooker. Do not push it against a wall.

MAINTENANCE

Like any other electrical appliance the microwave cooker should give years of trouble-free service providing it is used correctly. All manufacturers give guarantees and a number offer maintenance contracts. The choice of regular maintenance rests with the user but under no circumstances should anyone tamper with the cooker other than a fully trained microwave service engineer. If the removable base or turntable is broken by accident, it must be replaced by the manufacturer; a substitute should not be used.

RUNNING COSTS

Microwave cookers are very economical for the preparation of many foods, but there are occasions when it is cheaper to use a conventional cooker: if, for example, the conventional oven can be filled with food for a complete meal, or if you are batch cooking for the freezer.

A 500 watt microwave cooker used on the High setting will consume about 1 unit of electricity in 1 hour. A 700 watt microwave cooker will consume about 1 unit of electricity in 45 minutes when in use. The local Electricity Board can always advise on the cost of a unit of electricity.

CLEANING

The microwave cooker is easy to keep clean because there is no heat to 'burn on' splashes and spillages. Wipe up any spillage that occurs immediately after the cooking process is completed, as the microwave energy cannot differentiate between food being cooked in a container and food which has been spilt. Do not clean up during cooking because this will mean that the food is left standing and this could affect the end result.

The manufacturer's cleaning instructions should always be followed and under no circumstance should a cleaner be used unless it is recommended by the manufacturer. The interior of the cooking cavity should be cleaned after use by wiping it out with hot soapy water, then with clean hot water. If any stubborn spillage remains, do not use wire scouring pads or sharp implements such as knives. Generally, a soft bristle brush will help but failing this, heat a small quantity of water in the cooker because the vapour can help to soften the spillage.

As with all electrical appliances it is advisable to disconnect the microwave cooker before carrying out any major cleaning operation, but under no circumstances should the cooker be dismantled unless the manufacturer gives specific instructions for cleaning the turntable.

There may be occasions when you have cooked foods with a strong smell and even after cooking has finished the cavity will still smell strongly. If this happens, remove the odour by boiling a mixture of water and lemon juice within the cavity for a minute or two.

DESIGN

Microwave cookers intended for household use come within the scope of the Electrical Equipment (Safety) Regulations 1975 made under the Consumer Protection Act 1961. These regulations require domestic electrical equipment to be designed and constructed so that when in use it does not emit any kind of radiation that could be dangerous. The sale of any appliance which allows microwave leakage at a harmful level is an offence and the Electrical Equipment (Safety) Regulations are enforced by local trading standards authorities.

All reputable microwave cooker manufacturers ensure their appliances are safe and well insulated. However, as with all electrical appliances, a further guarantee of safety is the BEAB label of the British Electrotechnical Approvals Board. This means the appliance has been tested and approved for safety and leakage levels in accordance with British Standards.

DUAL ENERGY MICROWAVE COOKERS

There are a number of microwave cookers which incorporate other heating elements such as a grill. Many designs have the facility to be used purely as a small table-top conventional oven or as a microwave cooker. Whereas in other models the appliance is able to combine these facilities and either cook by using the speed of the microwave energy and then automatically finish off the cooking by a conventional cooking method, or they can use both the microwave and conventional energy, cooking simultaneously.

Each cooker manufacturer has designed the cooker using different element and microwave wattages. Because of the variations it is not possible to obtain cookery books to cover each appliance and the manufacturer's cookery book should be followed. However, such cookers can be used in conjunction with this book if using microwave cooking only. Where conventional cooking is included as a part of the recipe, experience will have to indicate if the dual energy microwave cooker can be used in preference to the conventional cooker.

COOKERY BOOKS

When choosing a microwave cooker it is worth looking at the manufacturer's cookery/instruction book to ensure that it covers the type of information which you are likely to need. Some cookery books have been written for other countries and give measurements in cups rather than imperial or metric quantities, while others may include ingredients which are not familiar or easily bought. Although this may be acceptable it is wiser to check before you buy the book.

DIFFERENT METHODS OF COOKING

Since microwave cooking is so different from the conventional forms, it helps to understand what is happening.

CONVENTIONAL COOKING

Heat is always required when cooking conventionally and is obtained from electricity, gas, coal or wood. The heat source may or may not be visible depending upon the construction of the cooking appliance.

Generally, the technicalities of cooking food are not even thought about but cooking food under a grill is using radiant heat, cooking food in an oven is using hot air convection currents, and cooking food on a griddle is cooking by conduction. When cooking conventionally it takes quite a long time for the food to cook because (a) large areas of the cooker and container have to be heated and (b) these methods of heat transference are very slow. In the microwave cooker the energy acts directly on the food, the cooker and container are not heated and the heat losses are kept to a minimum, so cooking by microwaves is often much faster.

MICROWAVE COOKING

Basically the principle is something like the energy picked up by a television set which is changed into pictures and sound, but the 'energy waves' for a

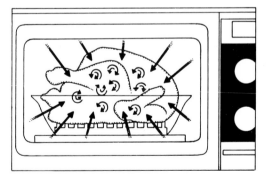

Vibrating molecules produce heat

microwave cooker are at a different frequency and are directed into, and contained within, a small box —the cooking cavity —with the result that they shake up the moisture molecules in the food. The molecules then vibrate at an enormous speed and this creates heat within the food which cooks it.

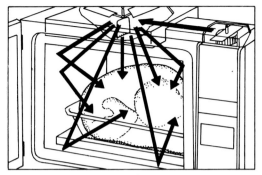

Built in stirrers circulate microwaves

Microwaves are invisible 'short' waves which are contained within the cooking cavity and are distributed by a **magnetron** which is built into the roof. They can be transmitted and reflected or absorbed.

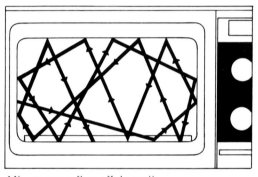

Microwaves reflect off the walls

They are reflected off metal and cannot pass through it, so the cooking cavity is always made of metal as this contributes to an 'energy pattern'. As the microwaves enter the cooking cavity, generally from the top, they are reflected off the walls, floor

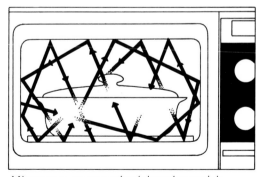

Microwaves are transmitted through materials

and door. They can be transmitted through other materials, rather like the warmth of the sun's rays can be felt through a window pane, so the microwaves pass through the food container and give their energy solely to the food.

Food looks solid to the eye, but under a strong microscope one can see that it is made of millions of moisture molecules. A sandy beach looks like a solid mass but when you go on to the beach you find it is made up of millions of grains of sand —it's a similar idea.

Microwaves are attracted to moisture and once food or liquid is placed in the cooking cavity the micro-waves will concentrate their energy on this and ignore the container material which can only get hot by contact with hot food. As the microwaves are absorbed by the food, the water molecules vibrate and create the heat which cooks the food.

Because microwaves are short waves, the greatest penetration is only 3.5–5 cm ($1\frac{1}{2}$–2 inches) all around the food. But what happens with thick joints?

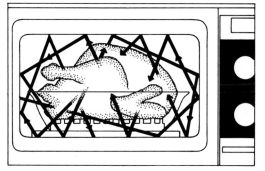

Heat continues naturally through joint

Because the first 3.5–5 cm ($1\frac{1}{2}$–2 inches) is so hot, the heat that has already been created will continue naturally through to the centre of the joint by conduction, just like cooking in the conventional manner.

MICROWAVE COOKER CONTROLS

All microwave cookers, whether basic or sophisticated, will have a timer and this is used for all cooking operations. Once the selected time is completed the control will automatically switch off the microwave energy. However, to check or stir the food, the door can be opened during the timed sequence and once closed will continue cooking for the remaining time. All cookers incorporate a cutout mechanism, so as soon as the door latch is released a fraction the microwave energy will stop being generated.

The basic cooker will have two cooking controls. One will supply the cooking cavity with 100% of microwave energy and may be termed as High, Full, Maximum or Cook. The second control is usually termed 'Defrost' and by using this the microwave energy is reduced to about 30%. This may vary from manufacturer to manufacturer so it is worth finding out from the manufacturer's book the energy or power available. By using this control large pieces or quantities of food can be thawed. It may also be used to slow down the cooking.

Other cookers may incorporate a variable power control. This control not only includes the maximum and defrost position but also gives a range of energy outputs enabling different cooking times to be selected to suit different foods. The power control may be marked in numbers or words such as High (100%), Medium, Low, Simmer, Roast, Reheat, Keep warm, and is usually achieved by pulsing the energy on and off for varying times. The pulsing times and technology vary from one manufacturer to another. So, it is not always possible to interchange recipes without some thought and experimentation. Nevertheless, recipes are supplied by manufacturers so that the benefit of the variable power can be enjoyed, provided recommended control positions and times are precisely followed.

HOW TO USE THE RECIPES IN THIS BOOK WITH YOUR OVEN

UNDERSTANDING POWER OUTPUT AND OVEN SETTINGS

Unlike conventional ovens, the power output and heat controls on various microwave ovens have yet to be standardised. When manufacturers refer to a 700-watt oven they are referring to the oven's POWER OUTPUT; its INPUT, which is indicated on the back of the oven, is double that figure. The higher the wattage of an oven, the faster the rate of cooking, thus food cooked at 700 watts on full power cooks at twice the speed as food cooked at 350 watts. That said, the actual cooking performance of one 700-watt oven may vary from another with the same wattage because factors such as oven cavity size affect cooking performance. The vast majority of microwave ovens sold today are either 600, 650 or 700 watt ovens, but there are many ovens still in use which are between 400 and 500 watts.

In this book

| HIGH | refers to 100% full power output of 600–700 watts.

| MEDIUM | refers to 60% of full power.

| DEFROST | is 30% of full power.

Whatever the wattage of your oven, the HIGH/FULL setting will always be 100% of the oven's output. Thus your highest setting will correspond to HIGH.

However, the Medium and Defrost settings used in this book may not be equivalent to the Medium and Defrost settings marked on your oven. As these settings vary according to power input, we have included the following calculation so you can estimate the correct setting for your oven. This simple calculation should be done before you use the recipes for the first time, to ensure successful results. Multiply the percentage power required by the total number of settings on your oven and divide by 100 to find the *correct setting*, e.g.:

Medium = % power required
(60%)   × total number of settings ÷ 100
        = correct setting, i.e.
        $$= \frac{60 \times 9}{100} = 5$$

Defrost = % power required
(30%)   × total number of settings ÷ 100
        = correct setting, i.e.
        $$= \frac{30 \times 9}{100} = 3$$

IF YOUR OVEN POWER OUTPUT IS LOWER THAN 650 WATTS, THEN YOU MUST ALLOW A LONGER COOKING AND DEFROSTING TIME FOR ALL RECIPES IN THIS BOOK.

ADD APPROXIMATELY 10–15 seconds per minute for a 600 WATT OVEN, and 15–20 seconds per minute for a 500 WATT OVEN.

ALWAYS CHECK FOOD BEFORE THE END OF COOKING TIME, TO ENSURE THAT IT DOES NOT OVERCOOK. DON'T FORGET TO ALLOW FOR STANDING TIME.

Some models include other features such as an interior cooking cavity light; menu and cooking guides in chart form on the front of the cooker which save time and effort in checking the cookery book whenever the cooker is used; browning plates and a probe which can be used when cooking meat and poultry to ensure the correct temperature is reached.

CHOOSING THE BEST METHODS OF COOKING

The size of the cooking cavity of a microwave cooker is small, especially when compared to a free-standing conventional cooker. Thus, the cooking cavity will restrict the quantity of food to be cooked. Just like any part of a conventional cooker, it can only cope with a certain quantity of food at any one time. For instance, if a saucepan is too small to use on the conventional hob then a larger saucepan is selected. The same applies to the microwave cooker. If it is too small to handle large quantities or takes too long to carry out an operation, then it makes sense to use the conventional method of cooking in preference to the microwave. The recipes in this book give reasonable quantities which result in fast, efficient cooking. If the quantities are increased then the cooking time will be longer.

At first, it was considered by many that the micro-wave cooker should be used for virtually every cooking operation. However, some food will look positively unappetising when cooked in a microwave cooker, though it will taste fine, while other food will just not cook correctly at all and some foods always look and taste better when cooked by conventional methods. So each cook must decide how and when to use the microwave cooker for maximum benefit.

The following summary gives a brief guideline as to which foods are suited to and which are not suited to microwave cooking.

FOODS WHICH COOK WELL

Soups, vegetables, fruit, preserves, sauces, hot puddings, cold desserts, poultry, many meats, pasta, fish, eggs (unshelled), suet pastry

FOODS WHICH COOK LESS WELL

Cakes, biscuits, dough mixtures, meringues, shortcrust pastry

FOODS WHICH ARE UNACCEPTABLE

Yorkshire puddings, hot soufflés, choux, puff and flaky pastry, roast vegetables

FOODS WHICH ARE UNSUITABLE

Deep-fried foods, eggs (in shells), fruit and vegetable bottling, casseroles

COMBINING METHODS OF COOKING TO BEST ADVANTAGE

In some instances it makes sense to use both the microwave cooker (for speed) and the conventional cooker (for external appearance, texture and taste). Some examples:

Cook sausages in the microwave, then brown under a conventional grill or on the hob.
Thaw and cook chips in the microwave, then crisp them on the conventional hob.
Thaw and/or cook frozen pastry pies in the microwave cooker, then brown in the conventional oven.
Thaw meat and poultry in the microwave, then cook conventionally.
Thaw and/or cook hamburgers or small cuts of meat in the microwave and then brown under the conventional grill or on the conventional hob.

Certainly, using both cooking methods in conjunction with each other can extend the use, range and acceptability of the microwave cooker by making the appliance work for the cook to save time and effort in food preparation.

Although the majority of recipes in this cookery course use microwave cooking methods, the conventional method of cooking has been included as a part of the recipe where it is considered a benefit to the final result.

SUMMARY OF MICROWAVE TECHNIQUES

The conventional cooker uses established methods to cook foods, therefore the terminology is long-standing. The microwave cooker uses new methods but to enable the user to understand the cooking process the same terminology is used. However, the method employed during the cooking process and the resulting cooked food may not necessarily be the same as would be achieved by using a conventional method. The following list gives basic information and more can be obtained at the start of each section of recipes in this book.

BAKING

Small quantities of cakes, biscuits and yeast doughs can be cooked but the result is not necessarily always acceptable. Browning does not occur and the colour and texture are different from the result obtained when cooking in a conventional oven.

Baking raw pastry is limited to shortcrust flan cases, although some cookers may be able to produce acceptable puff or flaky pastry strips for cream slices.

BOILING

If you require more than 600 ml (1 pint) water then it is more economical and quicker to use an electric kettle. Vegetables are successful but a minimum of water is required.

DEEP-FRYING

Deep-frying should not be carried out in the micro-wave cooker as there is insufficient control of the fat/oil temperature. Always deep-fry in the conventional manner.

GRILLING

As there is no radiant heat source in a microwave cooker you cannot grill food.

MELTING

The microwave cooker is very useful for melting or softening foods such as chocolate, fats, butter, icing and jellies.

REHEATING

Reheating is highly successful but like conventional reheating it is important that the reheated food reaches a very high temperature. When reheating slices of meat, always cover the meat with a sauce to avoid dehydration. Great care must be taken when reheating Christmas puddings, or pieces of Christmas pudding, since they dehydrate very quickly and the high sugar content can cause them to char. A cover is usually required but first check the cooker

Cooking meat with sauce

manufacturer's book for advice. It is advisable to watch small quantities of food and puddings carefully when reheating them. Reheating conventionally fried food is possible but the steam created within the product does result in the food losing its crispness, particularly food which has been fried in a batter.

ROASTING

This cooking method is quicker than using the conventional oven but it is essential to allow large joints and birds to stand for 15–20 minutes after its removal from the microwave cooker. If a higher degree of browning is required, it is advisable to brown the food, after microwave cooking.

SIMMERING

Unless the cooker has a low energy power setting, simmering cannot be achieved. However, if the microwave cooker has a Defrost (30%) control this can often be used for simmering.

STEAMING

Steamed foods are successful and cook fast as water is not required for the steaming operation. However, puddings require serving immediately or as soon as possible after standing and while they are still very hot since they tend to harden on cooling. Fish is successfully cooked in its own moisture.

STEWING

With good quality cuts of meat and poultry this can be achieved using High (100%). With cheaper cuts a satisfactory result can only be achieved using Defrost (30%). Fruit can be stewed very successfully.

THAWING

Most foods can be thawed in much less time than it takes conventionally but the manufacturer's instructions should be followed. Thaw large joints of meat and poultry completely before cooking.

LEARNING TO USE THE MICROWAVE COOKER

By following a few simple rules using the microwave cooker becomes a pleasure.

Read the manufacturer's instructions before trying the recipes.

Find out and make a note of the microwave output (wattage), for example 500, 600, 650 or 700 watts. This will be for the Maximum, Full or High setting and will use 100% of microwave energy for cooking.

Find out and make a note of the Defrost position. This will give less microwave energy than the maximum setting and is frequently referred to as a percentage, e.g. 30%.

Use virtually any container which can withstand the heat of the food but not one that is metal or decorated with metal.

If you are unsure about the timing, undercook the food as it can always be returned to the microwave cooker to complete the cooking.

Take things slowly and at first just use the micro-wave cooker for one recipe at a time. Trying to cook complete meals at first can be frustrating.

THE WATTAGE OF THE COOKER

All the recipes in this cookery book have been tested on a cooker of 700 watts output. If a cooker is used with a lower wattage, then increase the time by about 10–15 seconds per minute for 600 watt output cooker, and 15–20 seconds per minute for 500 watt output cooker.

TIMING

There are a number of factors which influence the cooking of food, for example whether the food and/or its container is porous or dense. Therefore, always check the food at the time given in the recipe and then at frequent intervals afterwards.

EGG SIZES

The size of an egg determines the amount of moisture and volume in a recipe. If smaller eggs than specified in the recipe are used then it may be necessary to increase other liquid measures.

QUANTITIES

The quantities given in the recipes may be increased providing the container can accommodate the quantity. However, it is recommended that any recipe containing a large amount of sugar should not be increased. Time is another factor to consider as it may be quicker to use conventional cooking methods for large batches.

COOKING CONTAINERS AND MATERIALS

Unlike conventional cooking, the microwave cook can use almost any type of container in the cooker. The exception is metal or containers which have metal as a part of their composition or decoration. Almost any non-metallic container may be used in the cooking cavity including glass, china, paper, basketry, linen and some plastics — as the container does not get immediately hot. The reason for this is that most of the materials that containers are made of do not absorb microwaves, so that the microwaves can pass straight through the containers without wasting any heat, and penetrate the food more quickly. The container may, however, become warm because the hot food will transfer its heat back to the container. The cooker manufacturer's instructions should always be adhered to but the following information will be helpful.

ABSORBENT PAPER

Paper table napkins and absorbent kitchen paper are useful for covering foods which may splatter but do

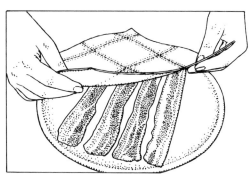

Covering bacon with kitchen paper

not require a complete cover. They are also useful when cooking toasted sandwiches or heating bread and pastry because by standing food on the paper the food is less likely to become soggy.

ALUMINIUM FOIL

Aluminium foil should only be used in *very* small quantities and in accordance with the manufacturer's

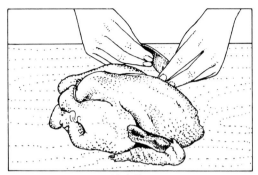

Mask poultry wings with foil

instructions. It must never be allowed to touch the cooking cavity walls or door. It is suitable for masking certain areas of food which might become overcooked before the rest of the dish is properly cooked, e.g. the tail of a fish, the bone at the end of a leg of lamb or the wings of poultry.

BASKET CONTAINERS

Basketwork containers can be used for a short time, for instance when quickly heating bread, but if they are used for too long, the material may lose its natural moisture and crack. Ensure that the basket is not constructed with metal staples or wire.

CARDBOARD CONTAINERS

Waxed cardboard containers should not be used as the wax could melt as the food heats up. Other containers are made specially for microwave use and have a special plastic coating. Cardboard cups and plates both have their uses: for example, cups can be used for individual puddings and cakes.

Paper cups for small cakes

CHINA CONTAINERS

Most china can be used in a microwave cooker, but mugs and cups with glued on handles are not suitable as the glue may melt with the heat from the food. Antique china and china with any metal ingredients or metal decoration should not be used. If a cover or lid is required for a dish, a china plate is a suitable substitute.

CLING FILM

Cling film is suitable for covering, wrapping and lining containers. If used, prick the film to avoid a build up of steam within the container, and when

Prick cling film

removing always pull back a corner furthest away from you to avoid being scalded by the steam given

Pull back cling film

off from the food. Alternatively, three-quarters cover the dish with cling film —this is more useful if you need to stir during cooking, otherwise you have to use a fresh piece of cling film every time.

GLASS CONTAINERS

Glass can be used providing it can withstand the temperature of the food being cooked or heated, but it is not recommended that antique, lead crystal or glass with metal decorations be used. A glass tumbler and a round container are useful substitutes for a ring mould. Simply place an inverted tumbler in

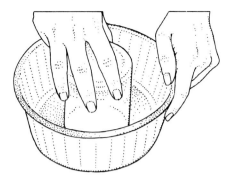

Making a ring mould

the centre of a round container and by changing the size of these two items many different sizes of ring mould may be obtained. If the glass tumbler is thicker than 0.5 cm ($\frac{1}{4}$ inch) this should not be used as it may break. This is because the temperature next to the food will be high and the temperature on the inside of a glass in a ring mould will be cold. This temperature difference could lead to the glass fracturing.

GREASEPROOF PAPER

Greaseproof paper can be useful as a covering, wrapping or lining for containers. Waxed paper is not suitable as the wax may melt from the heat of the food.

LINEN AND COTTON

Pure linen and cotton can be used for a short heating time: for example, when heating rolls or bread. A hot compress or Chinese hot serviette can be quickly prepared by wringing the serviette out in cold water, rolling it into a sausage shape and microwaving on High for about 1 minute.

METAL

Metal or metal-decorated containers should not be used. Some manufacturers recommend that small quantities of aluminium foil can be used for masking but always follow the manufacturer's instructions and never allow the foil to touch the walls or door of the cooking cavity.

MICROWAVE CONTAINERS

There are a number of containers available which have been specially designed for use in the micro-wave cooker. Many can also be used in the freezer and a conventional oven with a maximum temperature of 200°C (400°F) mark 6.

OVEN-TO-TABLEWARE

Oven-to-tableware, like china, can be used for a variety of purposes but should not be used if it has

metal as a part of its composition or is decorated with metal.

PLASTICS

Providing the plastic has been manufactured to withstand the heat of food, it will be suitable (such plastic is usually called thermoplastic), for example roasting bags and boil-in-the-bag bags. These should have the metal ties replaced with string or an elastic band, and the bag should be pricked to allow steam to escape. Some coloured plastics may not be suitable if the colour does not hold fast.

POTTERY AND EARTHENWARE

In general, these materials tend to be porous and often contain moisture within the container which will attract microwaves. This detracts from the amount of energy being absorbed into the food, so it will take longer to cook and the container could become very hot.
However, if a clay container is soaked in water first, it will absorb the microwave energy and slow down the cooking process, which takes longer to cook and produces tender results.

WOOD

Wood can be used but like basket work, must only be used for short heating times as the natural moisture from the wood may be lost and cause the wood to crack. Thick wooden skewers are suitable for kebabs and wooden cocktail sticks can be used for securing food. Lacquered wooden bowls should not be used.

SIMPLE TEST FOR CONTAINER SUITABILITY

1 Place a cup of water beside the container to be tested, in the cooking cavity.

To test for suitability

2 On high power, cook for $1\frac{1}{2}$ minutes.
3 Remove the cup and container.

CHECK

1 If the container is cool and the cup of water hot, then it is suitable.

2 If the container is warm around the edges and the water is lukewarm it is only suitable for short cooking times.

3 If the container is very hot and the cup of water is cold, then the container is unsuitable.

CONTAINER SHAPES

When cooking conventionally the choice of the shape and size of a container is generally automatic. For example, if making a 300 ml ($\frac{1}{2}$ pint) sauce it is unlikely that a 1.7 litres (3 pint) saucepan would be selected.

Using the most appropriate container in the microwave cooker, like a conventional cooker, will contribute to the best result. Some examples:

Do not use containers with acute corners. Vegetables such as peas or diced vegetables cook more quickly and evenly if spread over a shallow

Spread over shallow container

surface rather than piled into a small container. When thawing liquid foods select a deep container which keeps the thawed liquid close to the frozen block rather than one which allows the thawed liquid to spread.

Wherever practicable the size of the container has been specified in the recipes in this book. However, others may be used but it is important to select those which are of a similar capacity to ensure that boiling over will not happen.

Large bowl   = ovenproof glass bowl
             2.75 litres ($4\frac{1}{2}$–5 pints)
Medium bowl = ovenproof glass bowl
             2.1 litres ($3\frac{1}{2}$ pints)
Small bowl = ovenproof glass bowl
             1.2 litres (2 pints)
Small jug   = ovenproof glass bowl
             600 ml (1 pint)
Large jug   = ovenproof glass bowl
             1 litre ($1\frac{3}{4}$ pints)

COVERING AND WRAPPING FOOD

Microwave cooking is a different form of cooking so it will be helpful to have some indication as to when covers and wrappers are needed.

Foods which generally require a cover are those that need to retain the moisture, such as stewed fruit, vegetables, fish, soups, casseroles, hot puddings and when plated meals are being reheated.

Foods which need to be 'dry' such as cakes, pastries and bread do not generally require a cover.

When reheating cooked pastries, cakes and bread they do not require a cover but may benefit from being placed on a piece of absorbent kitchen paper.

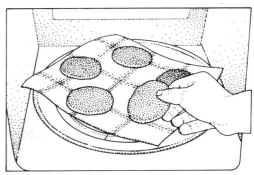

Arrange small cakes in circle

To avoid splattering from foods such as bacon and pork, cover with a piece of absorbent kitchen paper.

BROWNING FOOD

Microwave energy does not brown food in the same way as conventional cooking does. In many instances this is not important, but with certain foods such as meat and poultry, it is something which is preferable. If the meat or poultry is over 1.1 kg (3 lb) in weight, then some browning will occur, and it is possible to improve the colour of the poultry by brushing it with a brown sauce, for

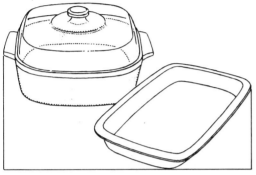

Use special containers for searing and browning

example soy sauce or Barbecue Sauce (see page 95), or use honey or brown sugar. There are also several commercial agents available which may be rubbed or sprinkled on to the surface of the food to give a more attractive finish. Nevertheless, for smaller pieces of meat and poultry (or for those who like the outside to be crispier) browning can be done in several ways. The microwave cooker can be used to do the cooking, then the food may be browned under a grill, in a frying pan or in the oven, just before serving. Alternatively, use a microwave browning dish or plate, which has a special finish applied to the base so that when it is heated in the microwave cooker it gets very hot, rather like a griddle. The uncooked food is placed on the base of the dish and it is seared and browned. The food is turned over and the searing is repeated before the food is cooked in the usual way. Most manufacturers recommend the use of a browning dish but check first and then follow the manufacturer's instructions carefully.

MICROWAVE COOKERY TERMS

There are certain skills you can use to obtain the best results from your microwave cooker.

BREAK UP
To speed up the thawing of foods such as soups and stews, break them up during the thawing operation.

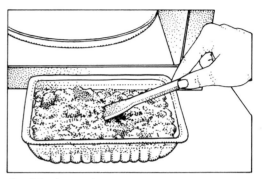

Break food up to thaw

DENSITY OF FOOD
Light porous foods such as cakes and bread will absorb microwave energy more quickly than food of the same weight which is dense and compact, such as meat and hamburgers.

FOOD ARRANGEMENTS
Arrange cakes, scones or other small foods in a circle. Avoid placing one in the centre. Arrange

Rearrange small cakes

foods with thinner parts such as chops, broccoli and asparagus, with the thinner or more delicate areas towards the centre of the dish.

Thinner parts towards centre

MOISTURE CONTENT

Liquids and foods which contain a lot of water will take longer to cook than those with a low moisture or water content.

QUANTITY OF FOOD

The more food put into the cooking cavity the longer it will take to cook. For example 300 ml ($\frac{1}{2}$ pint) milk could take about 3–4 minutes to heat, whereas 600 ml (1 pint) milk could take 5–6 minutes.

RE-ARRANGE

Small foods such as small cakes can benefit from being re-arranged at least once during cooking.

Rearranging small foods

TURN OVER

Foods such as joints and poultry benefit from being turned over halfway through cooking.

Turning joint over

TURN AROUND

Foods which cannot be stirred or turned over such as puddings and cakes, need the container turned around during cooking to ensure an even rise.

Turn during cooking

SEPARATE

Some foods such as fish fillets cannot be broken up but by separating the fillets as soon as possible during thawing, faster and more efficient thawing will be achieved.

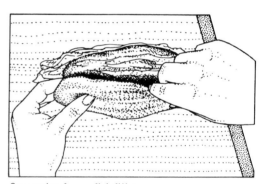

Separating frozen fish fillets

SHIELD

If the manufacturer's instructions allow you to use foil with your microwave cooker, use small thin pieces to protect some areas of food from over-cooking.

STANDING

Many foods, especially meat joints, poultry and cakes, benefit from standing after they have been removed from the microwave cooker as this time helps to finish off the cooking process. Wrap the meat in foil which, through the conduction of heat, cooks the centre. Sometimes the word 'resting' is used.

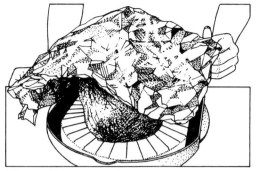

Wrap and leave to stand

STARTING TEMPERATURE

As with all methods of cooking, the colder the food, the longer it takes to heat and cook. For example, milk taken from the refrigerator will take longer to heat than milk which has been kept in the kitchen.

STIR

Stir liquid foods once or twice during cooking and always stir from the outside towards the centre.

Stir liquid during cooking

SUGAR AND FAT CONTENT

Foods which contain a high amount of sugar or fat will heat more quickly than those without.

THAWING

When food is frozen, ice crystals form, and these will vary in size from tiny to large crystals. Thawing should be carried out before reheating or cooking and the Defrost control should be used because if the frozen food is subjected to the full microwave energy, the small ice crystals would melt first, and the microwaves would concentrate on these. Consequently, the food could be partly cooked, partly thawed and partly frozen.

By reducing the energy or switching the microwaves on and off (pulsing), the warmth created during the 'on' time will spread to other parts of the food during the 'off' time; the result of this is a product that is evenly thawed. Most cookers have a Defrost control to be used for thawing.

The majority of the cooker manufacturers will give both charts and recipes for thawing, heating and cooking various types of food, added to which many food companies include or can supply instructions for cooking their products. However, the following information may be helpful in providing guidelines from which to work and you can note for yourself any limitations where they exist. More specific information can be found at the beginning of each section of this book.

BISCUITS

COOKING FROM RAW

Most conventional biscuit recipes do not cook well in a microwave cooker as they tend to spread and do not colour, so it is always better to use a microwave biscuit recipe.

THAWING

Care should be taken when thawing as overheating may spoil the biscuits. Arrange the biscuits in a circle on a piece of absorbent kitchen paper. One biscuit will take about 15 seconds on Defrost. Four will take about 30 seconds. Do not cover.

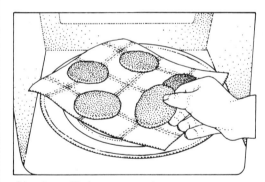

Biscuits on kitchen paper to thaw

CRISPING

If biscuits have become soft during storage they can be crisped up by microwaving. Follow the thawing instructions and once they feel warm set them aside on a wire rack to cool.

BREAD AND YEAST DOUGHS

COOKING FROM RAW

The physical size of the microwave cooker does not lend itself to cooking large quantities of dough. Therefore not more than 450 g (1 lb) should be cooked at any one time. The acceptability of the cooked dough depends on individual taste. It will be pale and have a soft crust. The colour may be improved by using brown flour and a crisp crust achieved by transferring the dough to a preheated conventional oven. A 450 g (1 lb) loaf will take about 5 minutes to cook on High.

REHEATING

Care should be taken when reheating doughs to avoid dehydration. Doughs should be removed when they are warm, not hot, to the touch. Reheating one roll takes about 15–30 seconds on High. Stand it on absorbent kitchen paper and do not cover.

THAWING

Like reheating, care should be taken. To thaw 1 slice of bread or a roll will take about 10–25 seconds on full power, and a large loaf about 8 minutes with a standing time of 10 minutes.

BOTTLING

Bottling fruit and vegetables is not advisable unless the cooker manufacturer gives specific instructions. Use the conventional method.

CAKES (see also page 113)

Microwave cakes cannot be compared to conventional cakes as they are a different texture and colour. Nevertheless, the speed at which cakes cook can be a bonus and once decorated, are equally attractive. A creamed cake mixture will take about 5–6 minutes to cook on High and a rich fruit cake about 50 minutes on Defrost. The cake should look slightly undercooked on the surface and this dries out on cooling. To test the cake, insert a warmed skewer or wooden cocktail stick. If it comes out clean the cake is cooked. After removing the cake from the cooker leave it to stand for about 10 minutes before turning it out.

Small fairy cakes should be arranged in a circle and checked frequently. Six would take about $1-1\frac{1}{2}$ minutes to cook on High. Do not cover.

THAWING

Generally, the Defrost setting should be used for a very short time and a long standing time is required. This could be from 20 minutes to $1\frac{1}{2}$ hours. For example, a cream sponge would need $1-1\frac{1}{4}$ minutes on Defrost plus a standing time of 25 minutes. Whereas a large cream gâteau needs 3 minutes on Defrost plus a standing time of $1\frac{1}{2}$ hours. Don't cover.

CHEESE

Like eggs, cheese is sensitive to heat, therefore care and attention must be given throughout cooking. It only requires very short cooking times and if overcooked will go stringy. Melting cheese on toast only takes about $\frac{1}{2}$–1 minute on High but it will not brown. Grated cheese is best added to sauces after the sauce has been made as the cheese will melt with the heat of the sauce. Cheese fondues can be made but they should be stirred frequently. On High 450 g (1 lb) cheese with wine would take about 6 minutes to melt.

RIPENING

Small quantities of cheese such as Camembert can be ripened using the Defrost setting; 75 g (3 oz) takes about 15–30 seconds.

CONFECTIONERY (see also page 123)

Using the microwave cooker means that small quantities are easy to cook and the risk of scorching is minimised.

DRINKS

Most liquids can be heated but it is important to select a container which will be large enough not to allow the liquid to boil over. Cups or mugs can be used. If more than 600 ml (1 pint) water is required it is quicker and cheaper to use an electric kettle. When heating spirits be very careful not to overheat them and watch them carefully. In many instances, it may be preferable to heat spirits in the conventional manner to ensure absolute control because they can catch alight if overheated.

THAWING

Set the control to High and break the frozen block up as soon as possible to speed thawing. Select a deep bowl which will keep the thawed liquid close to the frozen block. If the frozen drink is in a container, place it in a bowl of hot water for a few minutes. Remove the lid at both ends and push the block into a bowl, then microwave as instructed above.

EGGS

Eggs in shells should never be cooked as they 'explode' due to the build up of internal pressure. When cooking whole eggs both the white and yolk should be pricked before cooking. Eggs are sensitive

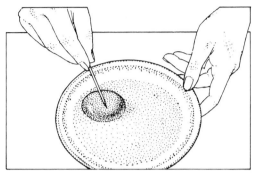

Prick egg yolk before cooking

to heat and therefore the cooking time is extremely short, it is always safer to follow a microwave recipe. Microwave omelettes are not to everyone's taste but a four egg omelette takes about $3\frac{1}{4}$ minutes on High with a standing time of 1 minute. Two poached eggs need about 1 minute on full power. Hot soufflés are best cooked conventionally as microwave soufflés look insipid and do not rise correctly.

FISH (see also page 41)

COOKING

Fish cooks beautifully in the microwave except for fried fish. One benefit is that odours are enclosed in the cooker and there is less likelihood of them permeating everywhere. When fish is cooked it should be opaque and flake easily.

THAWING

Fish should be cooked promptly, once it is thawed. Many commercially cooked products may be thawed and cooked simultaneously but the manufacturer's instructions should be followed carefully. The High power setting can be used but a more evenly thawed result will be achieved by using the Defrost setting. Note that 225 g (8 oz) of frozen fish will take about 7 minutes to thaw and cook using Defrost. Cover.

FRUIT

COOKING

Fruit retains its colour, shape and flavour and needs very little water in which to cook. For large quantities, i.e. over 900 g (2 lb), it is likely to be

quicker and more convenient to use the conventional cooking method.

THAWING

Frozen fruit can be thawed very quickly on High. If you wish the fruit to be served cold allow it to partially thaw, then leave it to stand. Remember that 450 g (1 lb) fruit takes about 5–6 minutes and should be left to stand for about 10–15 minutes. Cover.

REHEATING

Reheating can be carried out on full power but the fruit should be stirred to ensure even heating, 225 g (8 oz) takes about 4 minutes. Cover.

MEAT (see also page 60)

COOKING

Unless the piece of meat is over 1.1 kg (3 lb) it will not brown. Although microwave cooked meat is successful, much depends on individual taste. High can be used for both roasting and stewing good quality cuts but large joints will have an improved texture if a lower setting is used and many cooker manufacturers give these instructions. Cheaper cuts of meat are not successful unless a lower power setting is used.

THAWING/REHEATING

Thaw meat completely before cooking and then use at once. Do not use High for thawing meat, especially small pieces, since it will start to cook in the thinner places and yet still be frozen in the centre; it is preferable to use the Defrost setting. A 1 kg (3 lb) joint will take about 30 minutes to thaw and should be checked frequently to ensure that no part has started to cook. If necessary, remove the meat and give it standing time to complete the operation. Cover, unless instructions are given to the contrary. When thawing and reheating cooked meat dishes, such as stews, ensure that the container is deep so that the thawed liquid is close to the thawing block. Stir several times during the thawing and before serving, check that the meat has been heated to a high temperature. A stew made with 450 g (1 lb) meat will take about 25–30 minutes to reheat on High. Cover.

PASTA/RICE (see also page 84)

COOKING

Both pasta and rice can be successfully cooked but there is little saving in time when compared with the conventional method. The main benefit is that boiling pans of water are not needed and the container in which the pasta or rice was cooked is easier to clean.

THAWING/REHEATING

Frozen cooked pasta and rice can be successfully thawed and heated. Place the pasta or rice in a bowl and cover. Using High 225 g (8 oz) of pasta or rice will take about 6 minutes and should be gently separated with a fork halfway through the time.

PASTRY

COOKING

Generally it is best to cook all pastries in a conventional oven. Using the microwave cooker produces insipid and poor textured results. However, acceptable results can be achieved with shortcrust flan cases and puddings made with suet crust. Some cooker manufacturers do include pastry recipes in their instructions and successful results can be achieved if these are followed carefully. Remember that biscuit crumb flan bases are very easy and successful and could often be substituted for a shortcrust pastry case.

THAWING

Frozen pastry can be thawed quickly for use. Remember that 450 g (1 lb) pastry can be microwaved on High for $1\frac{1}{2}$ minutes, then left to stand for 20 minutes before using. A large meat pie takes about 5–6 minutes to thaw, but requires a standing time and finishing off in a preheated conventional oven. Do not cover.

REHEATING

Cooked pastry dishes can be reheated but often the pastry goes 'soggy'. If a very crisp pastry is desired then the conventional cooking method is more successful. Do not cover.

POULTRY (see also page 54)

COOKING

Poultry should always be completely thawed before cooking. Unless the bird is over 1.1 kg (3 lb) it will not be in the oven long enough for it to brown. Use High for roasting. Poultry cooks quickly and has a good texture and flavour.

Using a temperature probe is a sure way of checking the degree of cooking. The temperature required is generally between 82°C–85°C (180°F–185°F) and this temperature will increase once the bird has been removed from the cooker and is allowed to stand. If a microwave temperature probe or thermometer is not available, it is important to ensure that all the poultry is thoroughly cooked. To

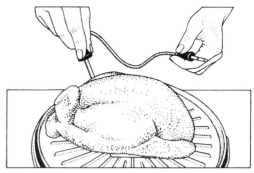

Using a temperature probe

do this, pierce the thickest part of the leg with a skewer; if the juices run clear then the bird is cooked. An ordinary meat thermometer can be used *after* the poultry is removed from the cooker, but under no circumstances should it be inserted into the poultry while it is in the oven.

REHEATING

Reheat cooked poultry dishes using High, but it is essential to check that the poultry is thoroughly reheated to a very high temperature. A frozen casserole using 4 chicken joints takes about 25 minutes to reheat. Cover.

THAWING

Raw whole poultry and joints should be thoroughly thawed before cooking; ice crystals should not be apparent, and the limbs should be flexible. Cook the poultry as soon as possible after thawing. Precise times are difficult to give for thawing as it will depend upon the weight and density of the poultry. Cooker manufacturers generally include instructions and these should be followed, but if the poultry has not thawed after the given time, leave it to stand, or immerse it in cold water. As a guide, a 1.1 kg (3 lb) chicken may take between 40 and 60 minutes to thaw completely and this will include a standing time. The Defrost control should always be used when thawing large pieces of poultry unless other instructions are given.

The poultry should be checked frequently during thawing to avoid it starting to cook. Cover the bird unless instructions are given to the contrary.

PRESERVES (see also page 116)

Preserving is very successful in a microwave cooker but it is important not to exceed the manufacturer's recommended quantities. The microwave cooker is only suitable for small quantities and if larger quantities are required then the conventional method should be used. Use the microwave cooker for sterilizing jars — it is easier than using the conventional methods.

SAUCES (see also page 92)

COOKING

Sauces are highly successful and microwave sauces can be cooked in the jug in which they are to be served. Furthermore, there is no risk of burning or scorching the sauce.

THAWING

Use High and break up the frozen block as soon as possible to speed up the thawing process. Select a deep container which will keep the thawed liquid close to the frozen block and cover. Using full power, 300 ml ($\frac{1}{2}$ pint) sauce takes about 6—7 minutes.

REHEATING

Reheating can be carried out on High but the sauce should be stirred frequently and the container should be large enough to prevent boiling over. It will take 300 ml ($\frac{1}{2}$ pint) sauce about 4—5 minutes to reheat. Do not cover.

SOUPS (see also page 27)

Soups are very successful in a microwave cooker since there is no risk of scorching and little washing up. Unlike conventionally cooked soups it is better to start with hot liquid rather than cold. Generally, only High is used.

THAWING

High can be used and the frozen block should be broken up as soon as possible to speed the thawing process. Select a deep container which will keep the thawed liquid close to the frozen block. Cover. On High 900 ml (1$\frac{1}{2}$ pints) soup takes about 25 minutes to thaw and heat.

REHEATING

Reheating can be carried out on High but the soup should be stirred frequently and the container should be large enough to prevent boiling over. On High 900 ml (1$\frac{1}{2}$ pints) soup takes about 9 minutes to reheat. Cover.

VEGETABLES (see also page 71)

COOKING

Vegetables retain their colour, flavour and nutrients as very little cooking water is used but if very soft vegetables are desired then the conventional cooking method should be used. For large quantities, i.e. over 900 g (2 lb), it is likely to be quicker and more convenient to use the conventional cooking method.

THAWING

Frozen vegetables can be thawed and cooked simultaneously using no extra water. On High, 225 g (8 oz) vegetables take about 6—7 minutes. Cover.

REHEATING

Reheating can be carried out on High but the vegetables should be stirred to ensure even heating. It will take 225 g (8 oz) vegetables about 3—4 minutes to reheat. Cover.

BLANCHING

Blanching vegetables for the freezer can be carried out but if the quantity exceeds 450 g (1 lb) then the conventional method is better. The preparation of the vegetables before and after cooking is the same for either method. Use High and the blanching will take about 3 minutes. The vegetables and 75 ml (3 fl oz) water are placed in a 2.75 litre (4$\frac{1}{2}$—5 pint) container and covered. The vegetables should be stirred halfway through cooking and then left to stand for 1 minute before plunging them into cold water. Overcooking results in starchy and less sweet vegetables. For details of precise times always check with the cooker manufacturer's instructions.

WHAT'S GONE WRONG?

Even the most experienced cook has the occasional disappointing result and cooking in the microwave cooker does not eliminate this. If it happens, it helps to know why the result is not as it should be so you can prevent it from happening again.

Baked apples, bursting	Either the apple skins have not been sufficiently pricked or scored; or the type of apple used had a high moisture content. **Remedy** Remove skins and purée in a blender or food processor; or cover with meringue and bake in a preheated hot conventional oven until golden brown.
Bread/rolls (reheated), hard on cooling	The food has been overheated. **Remedy** Use the bread or rolls to make breadcrumbs for coatings.
Cake, hard on cooling	Either the cake has been cooked for too long; or the container was larger than the one specified; or the specified quantity of liquid has been varied; or the eggs were not of the size specified. **Remedy** No remedy.
Cake, uncooked in the centre	Either the container was not of the correct size for the quantity of mixture; or insufficient cooking time was given; or the eggs used were larger than those specified; or the cake container was not raised above the cooker floor; or too much liquid has been used.

Remedy
Cut out the centre of the cake with a large pastry cutter and ice with butter or glacé icing; or use the cooked cake in a trifle; or crumble the cooked cake and add other ingredients to make a refrigerator cake or truffles.

Cake, unevenly risen	Either the uncooked mixture was unevenly spread in the container; or the container base was uneven; or the container has not been turned during cooking. **Remedy** Level the top by cutting with a knife. Turn upside down and use as usual.
Eggs, burst	The white and yolk has not been pricked. **Remedy** No remedy but edible if desired.
Eggs, only partially-cooked	Either the recommended size of egg was not used; or the container used was not the correct size; or the eggs were used straight from the refrigerator; or more eggs than specified were cooked without extra cooking time being given: or the standing time was insufficient. **Remedy** Scrambled: Continue to cook in the microwave; or discard watery liquid and eat the cooked egg if this is acceptable; or no remedy. Baked or poached: Continue to cook in the microwave;

or chop the cooked parts and
use in a salad;

or no remedy.

Jam, not set	Either insufficient cooking time was given;
	or the fruit was not high enough in pectin;
	or the quantities given in the recipe were exceeded.

Remedy

Return to the microwave and
continue boiling until
setting point is reached;

or use commercial pectin in
accordance with the
manufacturer's
instructions.

| Kidneys and livers, popping | Either the fine membrane (skin) was not removed before cooking; |
| | or the offal was not pricked. |

Remedy

Prick with a fork and
continue cooking.

Meat casserole or stew, meat/ vegetables not hot	Either insufficient heating time was given;
	or the food was not stirred during heating;
	or the liquid was boiling and the meat/vegetables were assumed to be as hot.

Remedy

Return to microwave and
cook until hot.

Check the meat or vegetables,
not the sauce.

Meat joint, undercooked on carving	Either insufficient cooking time was given;
	or insufficient standing time was given;
	or the meat was left to stand without being wrapped in foil;
	or the meat was not completely thawed before cooking.

Remedy

Arrange slices on a plate,
cover with a gravy. Cover
the plate with cling film

and cook until the desired
degree of cooking has
been achieved.

Stewed meat was tough	Either insufficient cooking time was given;
	or the meat was cut into larger pieces than specified in the recipe;
	or the power setting used was too high.

Remedy

Bring the stew to the boil on
High. Cook for 5–10
minutes. Reduce to
Defrost. Cook until
tender.

Pasta, hard or brittle	Either the cooking time was insufficient;
	or the standing time was insufficient;
	or the pasta was not completely covered with water during cooking.

Remedy

No remedy.

| Pastry pies, cooked and reheated, with soggy pastry | Either the pies were over-heated and the steam from the hot filling was absorbed by the pastry; |
| | or the pies were intended to be heated in a conventional oven. |

Remedy

Place in a hot preheated
conventional oven until
crisp. Be careful not to
overheat or the pastry may
harden.

Potatoes in their jackets, un-evenly cooked	Either the potatoes were incorrectly arranged;
	or the standing time was insufficient;
	or the potatoes were not wrapped in foil after cooking.

Remedy

Return to the microwave.
Cook each potato for
about 2 minutes. Wrap in
foil and stand for 5
minutes;

or scoop out the potato and beat with butter and milk using an electric mixer or food processor.

Poultry, under-cooked	Either the poultry had not completely thawed before cooking;
	or insufficient cooking time was given;
	or insufficient standing time was given;
	or the bird was left to stand without being wrapped in foil.
	Remedy
	Return to the microwave and cook until juices run clear;
	or cook under a conventional grill.
Rice, uncooked	Either the cooking time was insufficient;
	or the standing time was insufficient.
	Remedy
	Add more boiling water, cover with cling film and cook until tender.
Sauce, boiled over	The cooking container was too small.
	Remedy
	Transfer to a larger container and continue cooking.
Sauce, lumpy	Either the container in which the sauce was cooked was too large;
	or the sauce was not blended correctly before cooking;
	or the sauce was not stirred frequently enough during cooking.
	Remedy
	Pass through a sieve;
	or beat with an electric mixer;
	or liquidise in a blender.
Vegetables, hard	Either the vegetable was old and already lacked moisture before it was cooked;

or the stalks were not split;

or they were cooked for too long and dehydrated;

or more water than the recommended quantity was used, so that the energy went into heating the water not the food.

Remedy

If not totally dehydrated, mix the vegetables with stock in a blender or food processor to make a soup.

Sauce too sweet	Too generous with the sugar.
	Remedy
	Add a little lemon juice.
Jelly not set	Room too warm;
	or too much liquid.
	Remedy
	Put in refrigerator;
	or melt again and add more gelatine or jelly cubes.
Curry/Chilli too hot	Over generous with curry powder or chilli.
	Remedy
	Stir in a little soured cream, yogurt, lemon juice or instant potato.
Soup/Stew/ Casserole too salty	Too generous with salt.
	Remedy
	Cook a raw potato in it for about 10 minutes;
	or, if too acid, add a teaspoon of sugar.
Casserole/Stew or Soup too runny	Too much stock used;
	or insufficient thickening, such as flour, rice or cornflour.
	Remedy
	Add some instant potato;
	or mix some cornflour with a little cold water. Bring the mixture to the boil. Stir every minute.

SOUPS AND **S**TARTERS

MICROWAVE COURSE GUIDANCE

Use a container large enough to avoid the soup boiling over.

The best shape for a microwave container is one that is large, round and shallow with straight sides.

Remember as the cooking time is short less evaporation will take place.

Unless otherwise stated always cover vegetables, meat or fish with cling film, pulling back one edge to allow steam to escape, but do not cover once stock has been added.

Use hot stock in preference to cold.

Stir the soup several times during cooking.

If home-made stock is not used, use 2 stock cubes to every 900 ml (1½ pints) hot water to ensure a full flavour.

Do not add extra salt to the soup.

Freeze soup in small quantities for quicker reheating. Pour the soup into a freezer bag in the bowl you intend to use for serving.

CANNED CHICKEN SOUP

SERVES ▶ 2–3
SETTING ▶ HIGH
TIME ▶ $5\frac{1}{2}$ MINUTES
GRADING ▶ VERY EASY

450 ml ($\frac{3}{4}$ pint) can chicken soup

1 Put the soup in a 1.2 litre (2 pint) bowl. Cook, uncovered, for $5\frac{1}{2}$ minutes or until hot. Stir halfway through cooking.

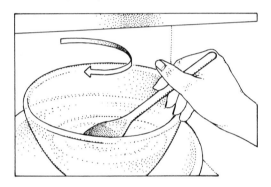

2 Pour into warmed soup bowls or mugs to serve.

——— TIPS ———

ANY CREAM SOUP MAY BE HEATED WITH A SIMILAR TIMING.

IF MORE CONVENIENT, DIVIDE SOUP AMONG MUGS OR SOUP BOWLS TO COOK.

IF USING INDIVIDUAL CONTAINERS USE A SIZE WHICH WILL AVOID THE SOUP BOILING OVER.

TO GIVE A LIFT TO THE SOUP A TABLESPOON OF DRY SHERRY CAN BE ADDED BEFORE HEATING.

CANNED VEGETABLE SOUP

SERVES ▶ 2–3
SETTING ▶ HIGH
TIME ▶ 7 MINUTES
GRADING ▶ VERY EASY

450 ml ($\frac{3}{4}$ pint) can vegetable soup

1 Put the soup in a 1.2 litre (2 pint) bowl. Cook, uncovered, for 7 minutes or until the vegetables are hot. Stir halfway through cooking.

2 Pour into warmed soup bowls or mugs to serve.

——— TIPS ———

IF MORE CONVENIENT DIVIDE THE SOUP AMONG MUGS OR SOUP BOWLS TO COOK IT.

IF USING INDIVIDUAL CONTAINERS USE A SIZE WHICH WILL AVOID THE SOUP BOILING OVER.

DEHYDRATED SOUP

SERVES ▶	2–4
SETTING ▶	HIGH
TIME ▶	12 MINUTES
GRADING ▶	VERY EASY

31 g (1.25 oz) packet dehydrated vegetable soup

900 ml (1½ pints) hot water

1 Put the soup powder in a 2 litre (3½ pint) bowl. Stir in the hot water. Cover with cling film, pulling back one corner to allow steam to escape and cook for 12 minutes. Stir halfway through cooking.

2 Re-cover and set aside for 5 minutes before serving.

3 Pour the soup into warmed serving bowls or mugs to serve.

——— TIP ———

THIS METHOD IS NOT LIKELY TO BE FASTER THAN THE CONVENTIONAL METHOD, ALTHOUGH AS A SAUCEPAN IS NOT REQUIRED SOME MAY PREFER TO USE IT.

CREAM OF VEGETABLE SOUP

SERVES ▶	4
SETTING ▶	HIGH
TIME ▶	10½ MINUTES
GRADING ▶	EASY

1 small onion, skinned and finely chopped

15 g (½ oz) butter or margarine

397 g (14 oz) can mixed vegetables, drained

10 ml (2 level tsp) cornflour

300 ml (½ pint) milk

300 ml (½ pint) hot vegetable stock

salt and pepper

chopped fresh parsley, to garnish

1 Put the onion and the butter in a 2 litre (3½ pint) bowl. Cover with cling film, pulling back one corner to allow steam to escape and cook for 4 minutes or until onion is tender.

2 Stir in the vegetables. Blend the cornflour with a little of the milk to make a smooth paste. Stir into the vegetables with the remaining milk, hot stock, salt and pepper.

3 Liquidise in a blender or food processor. Return to the bowl. Cook, uncovered, for 6½ minutes or until hot and thickened. Stir after 2 and 4 minutes.

4 Check seasoning. Pour into warmed soup bowls to serve. Garnish with chopped parsley.

SPINACH SOUP

SERVES ▶ 3–4
SETTING ▶ HIGH
TIME ▶ $15\frac{1}{2}$ MINUTES
GRADING ▶ EASY

1 small onion, skinned and finely chopped

25 g (1 oz) butter or margarine

25 g (1 oz) plain flour

300 ml ($\frac{1}{2}$ pint) milk

450 ml ($\frac{3}{4}$ pint) hot chicken stock

275 g (10 oz) can spinach, drained

salt and pepper

fried croûtons, to garnish

1 Put the onion and butter in a 2 litre ($3\frac{1}{2}$ pint) bowl. Cover with cling film, pulling back one corner to allow steam to escape and cook for 4 minutes or until onion is tender.

2 Stir in the flour and cook, uncovered, for 30 seconds. Gradually blend in the milk. Stir in the hot stock, spinach, salt and pepper. Cook, uncovered, for 8 minutes. Stir halfway through cooking.

3 Liquidise in a blender or food processor. Check seasoning. Return to the bowl. Cook for 3 minutes or until hot.

4 Pour into warmed soup bowls to serve. Garnish with fried croûtons.

PEA SOUP

SERVES ▶ 3–4
SETTING ▶ HIGH
TIME ▶ 17 MINUTES
GRADING ▶ EASY

1 medium onion, skinned and finely chopped

15 g ($\frac{1}{2}$ oz) butter or margarine

568 ml (1 pint) milk

two 275 g (10 oz) cans processed peas, drained

150 ml ($\frac{1}{4}$ pint) hot chicken stock

salt and pepper

30 ml (2 tbsp) single cream, to garnish

1 Put the onions and butter in a 2 litre ($3\frac{1}{2}$ pint) bowl. Cover with cling film, pulling back one corner to allow steam to escape and cook for 5 minutes or until onions are tender.

2 Stir in the milk, peas and hot stock. Re-cover and cook for 9 minutes. Stir halfway through cooking.

3 Liquidise in a blender or food processor. Season with salt and pepper. Return to bowl. Cook, uncovered, for 3 minutes or until hot.

4 Pour into warmed soup bowls to serve. Swirl a little cream on the top of each bowl.

———— TIP ————

IF A THINNER SOUP IS WANTED INCREASE THE QUANTITY OF STOCK.

MUSHROOM AND BASIL SOUP

SERVES ▶	4–6
SETTING ▶	HIGH
TIME ▶	17 MINUTES
GRADING ▶	LESS EASY

25 g (1 oz) butter or margarine

1 medium onion, skinned and grated

225 g (8 oz) mushrooms, finely chopped

25 g (1 oz) cornflour

300 ml (½ pint) milk

600 ml (1 pint) hot chicken stock

5 ml (1 tsp) chopped fresh basil

salt and pepper

1 Put the butter, onion and mushrooms in a 2.75 litre (4½–5 pint) bowl. Cover with cling film, pulling back one corner to allow steam to escape and cook for 7 minutes or until onions are tender. Stir halfway through cooking.

2 Blend the cornflour with a little of the milk to make a smooth paste. Add the remaining milk and stock.

3 Stir the liquids into the vegetables. Add the basil and season with salt and pepper. Cook, uncovered, for 10 minutes or until the soup has thickened and is hot. Stir after 4, 6 and 8 minutes.

4 Pour the soup into warmed serving bowls to serve.

——— TIP ———

THIS SOUP CAN BE LIQUIDISED AFTER COOKING IF A SMOOTHER SOUP IS WANTED.

BEETROOT SOUP

SERVES ▶	4–6
SETTING ▶	HIGH
TIME ▶	20 MINUTES
GRADING ▶	LESS EASY

400 g (14 oz) potatoes, peeled and diced

1 medium onion, skinned and chopped

400 g (14 oz) cooked beetroot, skin removed and diced

300 ml (½ pint) milk

450 ml (¾ pint) hot beef stock

salt and pepper

60 ml (4 tbsp) single cream, to garnish

1 Put the potatoes, onion and 45 ml (3 tbsp) water in a 2.75 litre (4½–5 pint) bowl. Cover with cling film, pulling back one corner to allow steam to escape and cook for 9 minutes or until vegetables are tender. Stir halfway through cooking.

2 Stir in the beetroot and milk. Re-cover and cook for 6 minutes. Stir in the hot stock.

3 Liquidise in a blender or food processor. Return to the bowl. Season with salt and pepper. Cook, uncovered, for 5 minutes or until hot. Stir halfway through cooking.

4 Pour into 4 warmed soup bowls to serve. Garnish each with a swirl of cream.

——— TIPS ———

IF THINNER SOUP IS PREFERRED INCREASE THE HOT STOCK BY 150 ml (¼ PINT).
THIS SOUP CAN BE CHILLED AND SERVED COLD.

CARROT AND HAM SOUP

SERVES ▶ 4
SETTING ▶ HIGH
TIME ▶ 20 MINUTES
GRADING ▶ LESS EASY

25 g (1 oz) butter or margarine

450 g (1 lb) carrots, peeled and thinly sliced

1 garlic clove, skinned and crushed

1 celery stick, finely chopped

1 medium onion, skinned and chopped

750 ml (1¼ pints) hot beef stock

salt and pepper

50 g (2 oz) cooked ham, diced

60 ml (4 tbsp) single cream, to garnish

1 Put the butter, carrots, garlic, celery and onion in a 2.75 litre (4½–5 pint) bowl. Cover with cling film, pulling back one corner to allow the steam to escape and cook for 11 minutes or until the carrots are tender. Stir halfway through cooking.

2 Add half the stock. Re-cover and cook for 5 minutes. Add the remaining stock.

3 Liquidise in a blender or food processor. Return to bowl. Season with salt and pepper. Add the diced ham. Cook, uncovered, for 4 minutes or until hot.

4 Pour into warmed soup bowls to serve. Swirl the cream on top of each bowl.

——— TIP ———

OLD CARROTS ARE NOT SUITABLE FOR THIS RECIPE AS THEY TEND TO DEHYDRATE AND TOUGHEN WHEN COOKED.

SEAFOOD SOUP

SERVES ▶ 4–6
SETTING ▶ HIGH
TIME ▶ 21 MINUTES
GRADING ▶ LESS EASY

25 g (1 oz) butter or margarine

1 medium onion, skinned and chopped

100 g (4 oz) leeks, trimmed and finely sliced

2 garlic cloves, skinned and crushed

15 ml (1 level tbsp) tomato purée

15 ml (1 tbsp) chopped fresh parsley

1 bay leaf

550 g (1¼ lb) filleted white fish, cubed

150 ml (¼ pint) dry white wine

50 g (2 oz) cooked mussels

50 g (2 oz) cooked cockles

50 g (2 oz) cooked prawns, peeled

450 ml (¾ pint) hot fish stock

salt and pepper

1 Put the butter, onion, leeks and garlic in a 2.75 litre (4½–5 pint) bowl. Cover with cling film, pulling back one corner to allow steam to escape and cook for 8 minutes or until vegetables are tender. Stir halfway through cooking.

2 Stir in the tomato purée, parsley, bay leaf, white fish, wine and 150 ml (¼ pint) cold water. Re-cover and cook for 6 minutes.

3 Stir in the mussels, cockles and prawns and continue cooking for 4 minutes or until hot.

4 Gently remove the fish and place it in a warmed serving tureen or bowl. Keep warm.

5 Add the hot stock to the liquid. Season with salt and pepper. Cook, uncovered, for 3 minutes or until hot, then pour the stock over the fish.

6 Pour the soup into warmed soup bowls to serve.

Opposite
Village Vegetable Soup (page 34)

MINESTRONE SOUP

SERVES ▶	4–6
SETTING ▶	HIGH
TIME ▶	23 MINUTES
GRADING ▶	LESS EASY

25 g (1 oz) butter or margarine

1 small onion, skinned and chopped

1 celery stick, chopped

1 carrot, peeled and sliced

30 ml (2 level tbsp) frozen peas

100 g (4 oz) cabbage, shredded

2 garlic cloves, skinned and crushed

15 ml (1 level tbsp) long grain rice

25 g (1 oz) macaroni

397 g (14 oz) can tomatoes, with juice

15 ml (1 level tbsp) tomato purée

600 ml (1 pint) hot beef stock

5 ml (1 tsp) chopped fresh parsley

225 g (8 oz) can baked beans

salt and pepper

1 Put the butter, onion, celery, carrot, peas, cabbage and garlic in a 2.75 litre (4½–5 pint) bowl. Cover with cling film, pulling back one corner to allow steam to escape and cook for 10 minutes or until vegetables are tender. Stir halfway through cooking.

2 Stir in the rice, macaroni, tomatoes with juice, tomato purée, hot beef stock and parsley. Re-cover and cook for 10 minutes. Stir halfway through cooking.

3 Stir in the baked beans. Season with salt and pepper. Cook for 3 minutes or until hot.

4 Pour the soup into warmed soup bowls to serve.

TOMATO AND CHICKEN SOUP

SERVES ▶	4
SETTING ▶	HIGH
TIME ▶	25½ MINUTES
GRADING ▶	LESS EASY

2 chicken breasts, boned and skinned, 175 g (6 oz) total weight

1 rasher streaky bacon, rinded and chopped

1 large onion, skinned and chopped

40 g (1½ oz) plain flour

300 ml (½ pint) milk

550 g (1¼ lb) tomatoes, skinned and chopped

15 ml (1 level tbsp) tomato purée

5 ml (1 level tsp) granulated sugar

450 ml (¾ pint) hot chicken stock

salt and pepper

1 Put the chicken on an ovenproof pie plate. Cover with cling film, pulling back one corner to allow steam to escape and cook for 3 minutes. Reposition halfway through cooking. Set aside.

2 Put the bacon and onion in a 2.75 litre (4½–5 pint) bowl. Cover with cling film, pulling back one corner to allow steam to escape and cook for 7 minutes or until the onion is tender. Stir halfway through cooking.

3 Stir in the flour and cook, uncovered, for 30 seconds. Gradually blend in the milk. Stir in the tomatoes, purée and sugar. Re-cover and cook for 10 minutes or until hot and thickened. Stir after 4 and 6 minutes.

4 Meanwhile, chop the cooked chicken. Add the hot stock and the chicken to the vegetables. Liquidise in a blender or food processor. Return to the bowl. Season with salt and pepper.

5 Cook, uncovered, for 5 minutes or until hot, stirring halfway through the cooking time. Pour into warmed bowls to serve.

Opposite
Mushrooms **G**reek **S**tyle (page 40), **B**aked **A**vocados with **H**am (page 40)

SUMMER APPLE SOUP

SERVES ▶	4–6
SETTING ▶	HIGH
TIME ▶	13 MINUTES
GRADING ▶	LESS EASY

800 g (1¾ lb) eating apples, peeled, cored and sliced

juice of 1 lemon

25 g (1 oz) granulated sugar

15 ml (1 level tbsp) cornflour

300 ml (½ pint) unsweetened apple juice

450 ml (¾ pint) hot water

salt and pepper

apple slices, dipped in lemon juice, to garnish

1 Put the apples, lemon juice and sugar in a 2.75 litre (4½–5 pint) bowl. Cover and cook for 8 minutes or until the apples are tender. Stir halfway through the cooking.

2 Blend the cornflour with a little apple juice to make a smooth paste. Stir in the remaining juice and hot water.

3 Pour the apple juice, water and cornflour mixture onto the apples. Liquidise in a blender or food processor. Return to the bowl and cook, uncovered, for 5 minutes or until hot and thickened. Stir every minute. Season with salt and pepper.

4 Pour the soup into warmed soup bowls to serve and garnish with apple slices.

——— TIP ———

COOKING APPLES CAN BE USED FOR THIS RECIPE BUT MORE SUGAR MAY BE NEEDED.

VILLAGE VEGETABLE SOUP

SERVES ▶	4–6
SETTING ▶	HIGH
TIME ▶	27 MINUTES
GRADING ▶	LESS EASY

25 g (1 oz) butter or margarine

100 g (4 oz) leeks, trimmed and finely sliced

100 g (4 oz) potatoes, peeled and diced

100 g (4 oz) carrots, peeled and finely sliced

½ green pepper, seeded and diced

50 g (2 oz) turnip, peeled and diced

2 tomatoes, skinned and chopped

150 ml (¼ pint) tomato juice

900 ml (1½ pints) hot beef stock

salt and pepper

1 Put the butter, leeks, potato, carrots, pepper, turnip and tomatoes in a 2.75 litre (4½–5 pint) bowl. Cover with cling film, pulling back one corner to allow steam to escape and cook for 15 minutes or until the vegetables are tender. Stir halfway through cooking.

2 Stir in the tomato juice, hot stock, salt and pepper. Re-cover and cook for 12 minutes or until hot. Stir halfway through cooking.

3 Pour the soup into warmed soup bowls to serve.

——— TIP ———

USE ANY COMBINATION OF VEGETABLE TO PRODUCE A SIMILAR STYLE OF SOUP.

CHILLED CUCUMBER AND COURGETTE SOUP

SERVES ▶	4–6
SETTING ▶	HIGH
TIME ▶	20 MINUTES
GRADING ▶	LESS EASY

350 g (12 oz) cucumber, peeled and cubed

275 g (10 oz) courgettes, trimmed and sliced

1 large onion, skinned and chopped

50 g (2 oz) butter or margarine

25 g (1 oz) cornflour

300 ml ($\frac{1}{2}$ pint) milk

450 ml ($\frac{3}{4}$ pint) hot chicken stock

salt and pepper

150 ml ($\frac{1}{4}$ pint) single cream

cucumber slices, to garnish

1 Put the cucumber, courgettes, onion and butter in a 2.75 litre ($4\frac{1}{2}$–5 pint) bowl. Cover with cling film, pulling back one corner to allow steam to escape and cook for 15 minutes or until the vegetables are tender. Stir halfway through cooking.

2 Blend the cornflour and a little milk together to make a smooth paste, then add the remaining milk.

3 Stir the milk and stock into the vegetables. Liquidise the mixture in a blender or food processor. Return to the bowl and season with salt and pepper.

4 Cook, uncovered, for 5 minutes or until hot and thickened. Stir every minute. Stir in the cream. Chill before serving. Pour into soup bowls and garnish with cucumber slices.

——— TIP ———

IF A SMOOTHER SOUP IS REQUIRED, PASS IT THROUGH A SIEVE.

CHILLED PLUM SOUP

SERVES ▶	4
SETTING ▶	HIGH
TIME ▶	10 MINUTES
GRADING ▶	LESS EASY

1 small onion, skinned and chopped

700 g (1$\frac{1}{2}$ lb) plums, quartered and stoned

25 g (1 oz) granulated sugar

pinch of ground cloves

salt and pepper

300 ml ($\frac{1}{2}$ pint) chicken stock

150 ml ($\frac{1}{4}$ pint) medium-dry red wine

1 egg yolk

150 ml ($\frac{1}{4}$ pint) single cream

1 Put the onion in a 2.75 litre ($4\frac{1}{2}$–5 pint) bowl. Cover with cling film, pulling back one corner to allow steam to escape and cook for 3 minutes. Stir in the plums, sugar, cloves, salt and pepper. Recover and cook for 7 minutes or until the onion and plums are tender.

2 Liquidise the plum mixture with the stock, red wine and egg yolk in a blender or food processor. Stir in the cream. Check for seasoning. Chill in a refrigerator.

3 Pour the soup into chilled soup bowls to serve.

HAM AND ASPARAGUS ROLLS

SERVES ▶	4
SETTING ▶	HIGH
TIME ▶	$4\frac{1}{2}$ MINUTES
GRADING ▶	VERY EASY

460 g (1.01 lb) can asparagus spears, drained

4 thin slices cooked ham

25 g (1 oz) butter or margarine, cut into four

pepper

thick mayonnaise and chopped fresh parsley, to garnish

1 Divide the asparagus into four bunches and place each on a piece of ham.

2 Dot each bunch with butter. Sprinkle with pepper. Roll the ham around the asparagus and secure with wooden cocktail sticks. Place the seamside of the roll downwards on a plate.

3 Cover with cling film, pulling back one corner to allow steam to escape and cook for $4\frac{1}{2}$ minutes or until hot. Re-position halfway through cooking.

4 Arrange the asparagus rolls on a warm serving dish and remove the cocktail sticks. Pipe or spoon a little mayonnaise over the rolls and finish the garnish with a sprinkle of chopped parsley.

MUSSELS IN WINE

SERVES ▶	4
SETTING ▶	HIGH
TIME ▶	$9\frac{1}{2}$ MINUTES
GRADING ▶	EASY

1 small onion, skinned and finely chopped

5 ml (1 tsp) chopped fresh parsley

25 g (1 oz) butter or margarine

5 ml (1 level tsp) plain flour

60 ml (4 tbsp) dry white wine

two 225 g (8 oz) cans mussels in brine, drained

parsley sprigs and lemon wedges, to garnish

1 Put the onion, parsley and butter in a 2 litre ($3\frac{1}{2}$ pint) bowl. Cover with cling film, pulling back one corner to allow steam to escape and cook for 4 minutes or until onion is tender.

2 Blend the flour with the wine. Stir into the onion. Re-cover and cook for 2 minutes. Stir halfway through cooking.

3 Stir in the mussels. Re-cover and cook for $3\frac{1}{2}$ minutes or until hot. Stir halfway through cooking.

4 Spoon on to warmed plates to serve. Garnish with the parsley sprigs and lemon wedges.

PILCHARD POTS

SERVES ▶ 4	
SETTING ▶ HIGH	
TIME ▶ 1½ MINUTES	
GRADING ▶ EASY	

100 g (4 oz) butter or margarine

45 ml (3 tbsp) lemon juice

425 g (15 oz) can pilchards in tomato sauce

pepper

parsley sprigs and lemon slices, to garnish

1 Cut the butter into pieces and put in a 600 ml (1 pint) jug. Cook for 1½–2 minutes or until melted.

2 Beat together, or use a blender or food processor, the melted butter, lemon juice, pilchards and pepper.

3 Spoon into 4 ramekins or small dishes and chill.

4 Garnish with sprigs of parsley and lemon slices. Serve with hot buttered toast if you wish.

ARTICHOKE HEARTS MAYONNAISE

SERVES ▶ 2–4	
SETTING ▶ HIGH	
TIME ▶ 3 MINUTES	
GRADING ▶ VERY EASY	

397 g (14 oz) can artichoke hearts, drained

2–4 tomatoes, sliced

90 ml (6 level tbsp) thick mayonnaise

parsley sprigs, to garnish

1 Arrange the artichoke hearts in a circle on an ovenproof dish. Cover with cling film, pulling back one corner to allow steam to escape and cook for 3 minutes. Stand, covered, for 2 minutes.

2 Arrange the sliced tomatoes on one side of each of 4 plates. Stand the artichokes next to the tomatoes. Spoon some mayonnaise over the artichokes. Garnish with sprigs of parsley.

TURKEY LIVER PÂTÉ

SERVES ▶ 4	
SETTING ▶ HIGH	
TIME ▶ 11 MINUTES	
GRADING ▶ LESS EASY	

3 rashers streaky bacon, rinded and chopped

1 medium onion, skinned and chopped

1 garlic clove, skinned and crushed

225 g (8 oz) turkey livers

*5 ml (1 tsp) chopped fresh mixed herbs or
2.5 ml (½ level tsp) dried mixed herbs*

100 g (4 oz) butter or margarine

30 ml (2 tbsp) double cream

salt and pepper

fresh parsley sprigs, to garnish

1 Put the bacon, onion and garlic in a 2 litre (3½ pint) bowl. Cover with cling film, pulling back one corner to allow steam to escape and cook for 5 minutes.

2 Stir in the livers and herbs. Re-cover and cook for 4 minutes. Stir halfway through cooking.

3 Cut the butter into pieces and add it to the livers. Re-cover and continue cooking for a further 2 minutes.

4 Stand, covered, for 3 minutes. Add the cream. Liquidise in a blender or food processor. Season with salt and pepper.

5 Spoon the pâté into 4 ramekins or small dishes. Chill. Garnish with sprigs of parsley. Serve with hot buttered toast if wished.

HOT PRAWN COCKTAIL

SERVES ▶ 4	
SETTING ▶ HIGH	
TIME ▶ 9½ MINUTES	
GRADING ▶ LESS EASY	

50 g (2 oz) butter or margarine

50 g (2 oz) plain flour

568 ml (1 pint) milk

15 ml (1 level tbsp) tomato purée

salt and pepper

275 g (10 oz) cooked prawns, peeled

15 ml (1 tbsp) chopped fresh parsley

whole prawns and parsley sprigs, to garnish

1 Put the butter in a 1 litre (1¾ pint) jug. Cook, uncovered, for 45 seconds or until melted. Stir in the flour and cook for 45 seconds. Gradually blend in the milk. Cook, uncovered, for 4 minutes. Stir every minute.

2 Stir in the purée, salt, pepper, prawns and parsley. Cook, uncovered, for 4 minutes or until hot.

3 Spoon into 4 small dishes. Garnish with whole prawns and sprigs of parsley.

CHICKEN AND CHIVE STARTER

SERVES ▶ 4	
SETTING ▶ HIGH	
TIME ▶ 14–15 MINUTES	
GRADING ▶ LESS EASY	

425 g (15 oz) chicken legs

25 g (1 oz) butter or margarine

25 g (1 oz) plain flour

300 ml (½ pint) milk

15 ml (1 tbsp) snipped fresh chives

salt and pepper

1 garlic clove, skinned and crushed

chive flowers or snipped chives, to garnish

1 Put the chicken legs in a 900 ml (1½ pint) casserole dish. Cover with cling film, pulling back one corner to allow steam to escape and cook for 7½ minutes. Re-position halfway through cooking. Set aside, covered, while making the sauce.

2 Put the butter in a 600 ml (1 pint) jug. Cook, uncovered, for 45 seconds or until melted. Stir in the flour and cook for 45 seconds. Gradually blend in the milk. Add the chives, salt, pepper and garlic. Cook for 4 minutes, uncovered. Stir every minute.

3 Remove the skin from the chicken. Finely chop the chicken flesh. Stir the flesh into the sauce. Check the seasoning.

4 Divide the mixture between 4 ramekins or small dishes. Cook, uncovered, for 1–2 minutes or until hot.

5 Garnish with chive flowers or snipped chives. Serve with hot buttered toast, if wished.

——— TIPS ———

ANY POULTRY CAN BE USED IN THIS RECIPE INSTEAD OF CHICKEN.
OMIT THE GARLIC, IF WISHED.

TARRAGON EGGS

SERVES ▶ 4	
SETTING ▶ HIGH	
TIME ▶ 3 MINUTES	
GRADING ▶ LESS EASY	

4 eggs, size 2, taken from refrigerator

90 ml (6 tbsp) double cream

5 ml (1 tsp) chopped fresh tarragon

salt and pepper

1 Break the eggs into 4 cocotte or small dishes. Prick the yolks with a cocktail stick. Cook, uncovered, for 2 minutes.

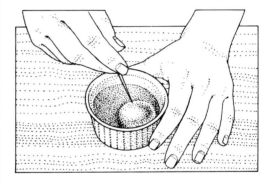

2 Mix together the cream, tarragon, salt and pepper. Pour the mixture over the eggs. Cook, uncovered, for 1 minute. Serve immediately.

——— TIP ———

IF SMALLER EGGS ARE USED THE COOKING TIME WILL BE LESS, SO CHECK CAREFULLY DURING COOKING.

MUSHROOMS GREEK STYLE

SERVES ▶ 4	
SETTING ▶ HIGH	
TIME ▶ $13\frac{1}{2}$ MINUTES	
GRADING ▶ LESS EASY	

30 ml (2 tbsp) olive oil

1 medium onion, skinned and chopped

2 garlic cloves, skinned and crushed

60 ml (4 level tbsp) tomato purée

5 ml (1 tsp) chopped fresh mixed herbs

300 ml ($\frac{1}{2}$ pint) hot vegetable stock

salt and pepper

450 g (1 lb) button mushrooms

chopped fresh parsley, to garnish

1 Put the olive oil, onion and garlic in a 2 litre ($3\frac{1}{2}$ pint) bowl. Cover with cling film, pulling back one corner to allow steam to escape and cook for 5 minutes or until the onion is tender. Stir halfway through cooking.

2 Stir in the tomato purée, herbs, stock, salt, pepper and mushrooms. Re-cover and cook for $8\frac{1}{2}$ minutes or until mushrooms are hot. Stir halfway through cooking.

3 Spoon the mixture into 4 warmed dishes. Garnish with the chopped parsley.

——— TIP ———

THE MUSHROOMS CAN BE SERVED CHILLED, IF WISHED

BAKED AVOCADOS WITH HAM

SERVES ▶ 4	
SETTING ▶ HIGH	
TIME ▶ $5\frac{3}{4}$ MINUTES	
GRADING ▶ LESS EASY	

40 g ($1\frac{1}{2}$ oz) butter or margarine

50 g (2 oz) fresh brown breadcrumbs

100 g (4 oz) cooked ham, finely chopped

90 ml (6 tbsp) double cream

dash of angostura bitters

salt and pepper

2.5 ml ($\frac{1}{2}$ tsp) chopped fresh parsley

2 large avocados

15 ml (1 tbsp) lemon juice

30 ml (2 tbsp) double cream and fresh parsley sprigs, to garnish

1 Put the butter in a 2 litre ($3\frac{1}{2}$ pint) bowl. Cook, uncovered, for 45 seconds or until melted. Stir in the breadcrumbs and ham. Add sufficient cream to bind the mixture, the angostura bitters, salt, pepper and parsley. Cook, uncovered, for $1\frac{1}{2}$ minutes.

2 Cut the avocados in half, remove and discard the stone, then sprinkle with lemon juice. Divide and pile the breadcrumbs mixture on to each avocado half. Arrange on a plate and cook, uncovered, for $3\frac{1}{2}$ minutes or until hot.

3 Place the avocados in warmed serving dishes. Drizzle each with cream and garnish with sprigs of parsley.

FISH AND **S**HELLFISH

MICROWAVE COURSE GUIDANCE

Unless instructions are given to the contrary always cover fish when cooking.

If cooking fish fillets overlap thin parts to prevent overcooking of the thinner ends.

When cooking steaks of fish arrange with the thinner ends facing in towards the centre of the container.

For whole fish, slash the skin in several places to prevent bursting.

Small pieces of foil can be used to protect the thin tail end of whole fish but be sure that only small amounts are used and that the foil does not touch any part of the interior of the cooking cavity.

Never attempt to fry fish in the microwave cooker.

Frozen fish can be thawed first in the microwave: put it on a plate and cook on Defrost, turning frequently.

Fish in batter which has been fried conventionally does not reheat well as the batter goes soggy.

Fish is cooked when the flesh flakes easily and is opaque. Overcooking fish will toughen the flesh.

When cooking shellfish, test frequently to prevent overcooking.

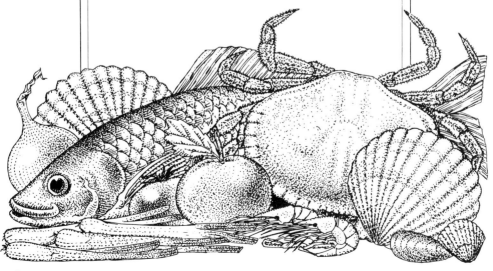

BASIC BUTTERED FISH

SERVES ▶ 2 or 4	
SETTING ▶ HIGH	
TIME ▶ Depends on cut of fish (see chart below)	
GRADING ▶ EASY	

450 g (1 lb) fish

25 g (1 oz) butter or margarine, cut into pieces (optional)

1 Arrange the fish in a shallow container with the thin parts of the steaks facing the centre. Arrange rolled fillets in a circle around the outer edge of the container. Position fillets overlapping or with the thin tail ends tucked under. Position whole fish with small pieces of foil protecting the tail end.

2 Cook covered. Allow:
Fish steaks, e.g. haddock, cod, salmon
4–5 minutes per 450 g (1 lb)
Standing time covered
3–5 minutes
Thick fish fillets, e.g. haddock, cod
5–6 minutes per 450 g (1 lb)
Standing time covered
4–5 minutes
Thin fish fillets, e.g. plaice, sole (rolled)
4–5 minutes per 450 g (1 lb)
Standing time covered
3–5 minutes
Fish fillets, e.g. plaice, sole (not rolled)
3–4 minutes per 450 g (1 lb)
Standing time covered
3–5 minutes
Whole fish, e.g. trout, salmon, herring, mackerel
4–5 minutes per 450 g (1 lb)
Standing time covered
5–10 minutes
A very large fish will require a longer standing time.

3 Dot the fish with butter, if being used. Cover with cling film, pulling back one corner to allow steam to escape and cook. If necessary, re-arrange, turn around or turn over halfway through cooking.

4 Allow the appropriate standing time. The fish is cooked when the flesh flakes easily and is opaque.

STUFFED SOLE FILLETS WITH CREAMY SAUCE

SERVES ▶ 2	
SETTING ▶ HIGH	
TIME ▶ 8 MINUTES	
GRADING ▶ LESS EASY	

25 g (1 oz) fresh white breadcrumbs

5 ml (1 tsp) chopped fresh thyme

salt and pepper

75 ml (5 tbsp) fish stock

4 fillets lemon sole, total weight 350 g (12 oz), skinned

25 g (1 oz) butter or margarine

15 ml (1 level tbsp) tomato purée

100 ml (4 fl oz) double cream

boiled rice, to serve (see page 86)

1 Mix together the breadcrumbs, thyme, salt, pepper and stock. Arrange the fillets with the skinned side uppermost. Divide and spread the stuffing over the fillets. Turn in the thin ends of the fillets to neaten. Roll up and if necessary secure with wooden cocktail sticks.

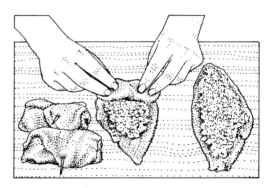

2 Place the fillets in a circle on an ovenproof pie plate. Dot each with butter. Cover with cling film, pulling back one corner to allow steam to escape and cook for 5 minutes. Pour the butter into a 600 ml (1 pint) jug. Keep the fish warm.

3 Stir the tomato purée and cream into the butter. Cook, uncovered, for 3 minutes. Stir halfway through cooking. Serve the fillets on a bed of cooked rice. Pour a little sauce over each fillet.

*F*ISH *K*EBABS

SERVES ▶ 4	
SETTING ▶ HIGH	
TIME ▶ $8\frac{3}{4}$ MINUTES	
GRADING ▶ LESS EASY	

2 courgettes, cut into 8 chunks

4 large mushrooms, stalks removed

550 g ($1\frac{1}{4}$ lb) monkfish, skinned, cut into 8 cubes

4 lemon slices

25 g (1 oz) butter or margarine

5 ml (1 tsp) chopped fresh dill or 1.25 ml ($\frac{1}{4}$ level tsp) dried

2 tomatoes, halved

boiled rice (see page 86) and Anchovy Sauce (see page 93), to serve

1 On each of 4 wooden skewers place a piece of courgette, a mushroom, a piece of monkfish, a slice of lemon, a piece of monkfish and a piece of courgette.

2 Put the butter and dill in a 1.2 litre (2 pint) bowl. Cook, uncovered, for 45 seconds or until melted. Brush the prepared kebabs with the melted butter and place on a plate. Cook, uncovered, for 4 minutes.

3 Baste the kebabs, re-arrange and push half a tomato on to each skewer. Cook, uncovered, for 4 minutes or until tender. Check and re-position halfway through cooking. Serve on a bed of boiled rice with Anchovy Sauce.

*C*OD *S*TEAKS WITH *S*HRIMP *S*AUCE

SERVES ▶ 4	
SETTING ▶ HIGH	
TIME ▶ $12\frac{3}{4}$ MINUTES	
GRADING ▶ EASY	

4 cod steaks, 175 g (6 oz) each, skinned

50 g (2 oz) butter or margarine

25 g (1 oz) plain flour

300 ml ($\frac{1}{2}$ pint) milk

2.5 ml ($\frac{1}{2}$ tsp) anchovy essence

salt and pepper

50 g (2 oz) cooked shrimps or prawns, peeled

fresh whole shrimps or chopped fresh parsley, to garnish

1 Arrange the cod steaks in a shallow container with the thin ends to the centre. Cover with cling film, pulling back one corner to allow steam to escape and cook for 4 minutes.

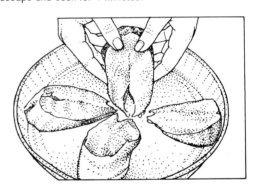

2 Turn the fish over and dot with 25 g (1 oz) of the butter. Re-cover and continue cooking for 2 minutes, then set aside, covered.

3 Put the remaining butter in a 600 ml (1 pint) jug. Cook, uncovered, for 45 seconds or until melted. Stir in the flour and cook, uncovered, for 30 seconds. Gradually blend in the milk and anchovy essence. Cook for 4 minutes or until thickened. Stir every minute.

4 Season with salt and pepper. Stir in the shrimps and cook for $1\frac{1}{2}$ minutes.

5 Arrange the steaks on a warmed serving dish. Pour the sauce over and garnish.

SMOKED TROUT MOUSSE

SERVES ▶ 4	
SETTING ▶ HIGH	
TIME ▶ 3 MINUTES	
GRADING ▶ LESS EASY	

1 fish stock cube, crumbled

25 g (1 oz) aspic jelly powder

450 g (1 lb) smoked trout, skinned and bones removed

15 ml (1 tbsp) double cream

salt and pepper

2 egg whites

lemon slices and parsley sprigs, to garnish

1 Put the stock cube and 300 ml (½ pint) water in a 600 ml (1 pint) jug. Cook, uncovered, for 3 minutes or until hot. Stir well to dissolve the stock cube.

2 Stir in the aspic jelly powder until it is completely dissolved.

3 Mash the fish with a fork. Stir in the cream. Season with salt and pepper. Stir into the aspic jelly and allow the mixture to cool.

4 Whisk the egg whites until stiff. Fold into the fish mixture. Spoon into a 750 ml (1¼ pint) ring mould. Chill until set.

5 Turn out on to a serving dish. Garnish with lemon slices and parsley sprigs.

TOMATO FISH PIE

SERVES ▶ 4	
SETTING ▶ HIGH	
TIME ▶ 25¾ MINUTES	
GRADING ▶ LESS EASY	

450 g (1 lb) cod fillet, skinned

700 g (1½ lb) potatoes, peeled and cubed

25 g (1 oz) butter

25 g (1 oz) plain flour

300 ml (½ pint) milk, plus 30 ml (2 tbsp)

5 ml (1 tsp) chopped fresh parsley

50 g (2 oz) cooked prawns, peeled

salt and pepper

30 ml (2 level tbsp) tomato purée

parsley sprigs, to garnish

1 Put the fish in a 2.75 litre (4½–5 pint) bowl. Cover with cling film, pulling back one corner to allow steam to escape and cook for 6 minutes. Re-position halfway through cooking. Set aside, covered.

2 Put 15 ml (1 tbsp) water and the potatoes in a 2.75 litre (4½–5 pint) bowl. Cover with cling film, pulling back one corner to allow steam to escape and cook for 10 minutes. Set aside, covered.

3 Put the butter in a 600 ml (1 pint) jug. Cook, uncovered, for 45 seconds or until melted. Stir in the flour. Cook, uncovered, for 30 seconds. Gradually blend in the 300 ml (½ pint) milk and parsley. Cook for 4 minutes or until thick. Stir every minute. Stir in the prawns.

4 Flake the fish, removing any bones. Stir the flesh into the sauce. Season with salt and pepper.

5 Mash the potatoes with the purée and 30 ml (2 tbsp) milk. Season with salt and pepper.

6 Pour the fish mixture into an ovenproof 1.2 litre (2 pint) casserole dish. Spread the mashed potatoes over the top of the fish, and mark with a fork to make a pattern.

7 Cook, uncovered, for 4 minutes or until hot. If wished, brown the potato under a preheated grill. Garnish with parsley sprigs.

HUSS WITH MUSTARD

SERVES ▶	4
SETTING ▶	HIGH
TIME ▶	8 MINUTES
GRADING ▶	EASY

900 g (2 lb) huss, skinned and cut into 4 pieces

25 g (1 oz) butter or margarine, cut into 4 pieces

15 ml (1 level tbsp) mustard powder

60 ml (4 tbsp) single cream or milk

45 ml (3 tbsp) chopped fresh parsley

salt and pepper

watercress, to garnish

1 Put the huss in a shallow casserole dish and dot with butter. Cover with cling film, pulling back one corner to allow steam to escape and cook for 6 minutes. Re-position and baste halfway through the cooking.

2 Mix together the mustard, cream, parsley, salt and pepper. Drain the butter from the fish and add to the mustard mixture. Pour the mustard mixture over the fish. Re-cover and cook for 2 minutes or until hot. Serve garnished with watercress.

STUFFED HERRINGS WITH CAPER SAUCE

SERVES ▶	4
SETTING ▶	HIGH
TIME ▶	$15\frac{1}{4}$ MINUTES
GRADING ▶	LESS EASY

1 small onion, skinned and finely chopped

5 ml (1 tsp) chopped fresh mixed herbs or 2.5 ml ($\frac{1}{2}$ level tsp) dried

25 g (1 oz) fresh white breadcrumbs

25 g (1 oz) fresh brown breadcrumbs

salt and pepper

2 eggs, size 2

4 herrings, each 125 g ($4\frac{1}{2}$ oz), skinned, cleaned and heads removed

25 g (1 oz) butter or margarine

25 g (1 oz) plain flour

300 ml ($\frac{1}{2}$ pint) milk

15 ml (1 level tbsp) chopped capers

parsley sprigs, to garnish

1 Put the onion and herbs in a 1.2 litre (2 pint) bowl. Cover with cling film, pulling back one corner to allow steam to escape and cook for 4 minutes or until onions are tender. Stir in the breadcrumbs, salt and pepper. Lightly beat 1 of the eggs and use to bind the mixture together.

2 Fill each herring with the stuffing. Roll up and secure with wooden cocktail sticks. Put the herrings in a shallow dish. Cover with cling film, pulling back one corner to allow steam to escape and cook for 6 minutes. Re-position halfway through. Set aside, covered, while making the sauce.

3 Put the butter in a 600 ml (1 pint) jug. Cook, uncovered, for 45 seconds until melted. Stir in the flour and cook, uncovered, for 30 seconds. Gradually blend in the milk. Cook, uncovered, for 4 minutes or until thick. Stir every minute. Beat the remaining egg into the hot sauce. Stir in the capers.

4 Arrange the herrings on a warmed serving dish and pour a little sauce over each one. Garnish with parsley. Serve the remaining sauce separately.

SMOKED HADDOCK WITH EGG SAUCE

SERVES ▶	4
SETTING ▶	HIGH
TIME ▶	12¾ MINUTES
GRADING ▶	EASY

4 smoked haddock fillets, 700 g (1½ lb) total weight, skinned

25 g (1 oz) butter or margarine

25 g (1 oz) plain flour

300 ml (½ pint) milk

salt and pepper

1 hard-boiled egg, chopped

chopped fresh parsley, to garnish

1 Arrange the fillets, overlapping if necessary, in a shallow casserole dish. Cover with cling film, pulling back one corner to allow steam to escape and cook for 6 minutes. Re-position halfway through cooking. Set aside, covered, while making the sauce.

2 Put the butter in a 600 ml (1 pint) jug. Cook, uncovered, for 45 seconds or until melted. Stir in the flour and cook for 30 seconds. Gradually blend in the milk. Cook, uncovered, for 4 minutes or until thickened. Stir every minute.

3 Season with salt and pepper. Stir in the chopped egg. Cook, uncovered, for 1 minute.

4 Arrange the haddock on a warmed serving dish. Spoon the sauce over the haddock. Garnish with chopped parsley.

HADDOCK CASSEROLE

SERVES ▶	4
SETTING ▶	HIGH
TIME ▶	13½ MINUTES
GRADING ▶	LESS EASY

25 g (1 oz) butter or margarine

1 medium onion, skinned and finely chopped

1 celery stick, finely chopped

175 g (6 oz) carrot, peeled and finely sliced

1 garlic clove, skinned and crushed

550 g (1¼ lb) haddock fillet, skinned and cut into pieces

5 ml (1 tsp) chopped fresh basil or 2.5 ml (½ level tsp) dried

450 g (1 lb) tomatoes, skinned and chopped

150 ml (¼ pint) hot fish stock

salt and pepper

15–30 ml (1–2 tbsp) single cream or milk

basil sprigs, to garnish

1 Put the butter, onion, celery, carrot and garlic in a 2.75 litre (4½–5 pint) bowl. Cover with cling film, pulling back one corner to allow steam to escape and cook for 6 minutes or until the vegetables are tender. Stir halfway through cooking.

2 Stir in the fillet pieces and basil. Re-cover and cook for 4 minutes. Stir halfway through.

3 Stir in the tomatoes, hot stock, salt and pepper. Cook, uncovered, for 3½ minutes or until hot. Cool slightly and stir in cream to taste.

4 Spoon into a warm serving dish. Garnish with fresh basil sprigs.

MACKEREL WITH FRESH GOOSEBERRY SAUCE

SERVES ▶ 4	
SETTING ▶ HIGH	
TIME ▶ 16–18 MINUTES	
GRADING ▶ LESS EASY	

50 g (2 oz) butter or margarine, cut into 4

4 small mackerel, 275 g (10 oz) each, skinned, cleaned and heads removed

salt and pepper

lemon slices and fresh parsley sprigs, to garnish

Sauce:

350 g (12 oz) gooseberries, topped and tailed

20 g ($\frac{3}{4}$ oz) cornflour

40 g (1$\frac{1}{2}$ oz) caster sugar

1 Spread a piece of butter inside each fish and season with salt and pepper. Arrange the mackerel in a shallow dish. Cover with cling film, pulling back one corner to allow steam to escape and cook for 6–8 minutes. Re-position halfway through cooking. Set aside, covered, while making the sauce.

2 Put the gooseberries and 100 ml (4 fl oz) water in a 2.75 litre (4$\frac{1}{2}$–5 pint) bowl. Cover with cling film, pulling back one corner to allow steam to escape and cook for 5 minutes or until tender. Stir halfway through cooking. Liquidise in a blender or food processor, then rub through a sieve.

3 Blend the cornflour with 45 ml (3 tbsp) water to a smooth paste. Stir into the gooseberry purée with the sugar. Cook, uncovered, for 3 minutes or until hot. Stir halfway through cooking.

4 Arrange the mackerel on a warmed serving dish. Spoon the sauce over each mackerel. Garnish with slices of lemon and parsley sprigs.

CURRIED COLEY

SERVES ▶ 4	
SETTING ▶ HIGH	
TIME ▶ 29 MINUTES	
GRADING ▶ LESS EASY	

700 g (1$\frac{1}{2}$ lb) coley fillets, skinned and cut into pieces

1 small apple, peeled, cored and chopped

1 small carrot, peeled and sliced

1 medium onion, skinned and chopped

65 g (2$\frac{1}{2}$ oz) butter or margarine

25 ml (1$\frac{1}{2}$ level tbsp) plain flour

225 g (8 oz) can chopped tomatoes with juice

300 ml ($\frac{1}{2}$ pint) hot fish stock

5 ml (1 tsp) lemon juice

1.25 ml ($\frac{1}{4}$ level tsp) ground cumin

15 ml (1 level tbsp) medium curry powder

15 ml (1 level tbsp) chutney

40 g (1$\frac{1}{2}$ oz) long grain rice

chopped fresh parsley, to garnish

1 Put the coley in a 2 litre (3$\frac{1}{2}$ pint) bowl. Cover with cling film, pulling back one corner to allow steam to escape and cook for 4$\frac{1}{2}$ minutes. Set aside, covered.

2 Meanwhile, put the apple, carrot, onion and butter in a 2.75 litre (4$\frac{1}{2}$–5 pint) bowl. Cover with cling film, pulling back one corner to allow steam to escape and cook for 6 minutes or until vegetables are tender. Stir halfway through cooking.

3 Stir in the flour and cook, uncovered, for 30 seconds. Gradually blend in the tomatoes and juice. Stir in the hot stock, lemon juice, cumin, curry powder, chutney and rice. Re-cover and cook for 13 minutes. Stir halfway through cooking.

4 Add the fish and liquid from the fish. Re-cover and cook for 5 minutes or until hot.

5 Pile on to a warmed serving dish. Garnish with chopped parsley.

——— TIPS ———

THE AMOUNT OF CURRY POWDER IN THIS RECIPE WILL PRODUCE A MILD CURRY —ADJUST IT TO PERSONAL TASTE. USE ANY WHITE FISH INSTEAD OF COLEY IF PREFERRED.

SCALLOPS WITH TOMATO SAUCE

SERVES ▶ 4	
SETTING ▶ HIGH	
TIME ▶ 17½ MINUTES	
GRADING ▶ LESS EASY	

*450 g (1 lb) potatoes, peeled and cut into
2.5 cm (1 inch) cubes*

salt and pepper

100 g (4 oz) button mushrooms, sliced

2 garlic cloves, skinned and crushed

50 g (2 oz) butter or margarine

25 g (1 oz) plain flour

150 ml (¼ pint) dry white wine

1 egg yolk

4 large scallops, sliced

25 ml (1½ level tbsp) tomato purée

25 ml (1½ level tbsp) double cream

15 ml (1 tbsp) milk

chopped fresh parsley, to garnish

1 Put the potatoes in a 2 litre (3½ pint) bowl with 45 ml (3 tbsp) water and a pinch of salt. Cover with cling film, pulling back one corner to allow steam to escape and cook for 8 minutes, stir after 4 minutes. Set aside, covered.

2 Put the mushrooms, garlic and 25 g (1 oz) butter in a 2 litre (3½ pint) bowl. Cover with cling film, pulling back one corner to allow steam to escape and cook for 3 minutes or until the mushrooms are tender. Stir in the flour and cook, uncovered, for 30 seconds. Gradually stir in the wine. Cook, uncovered, for 2 minutes.

3 Beat in the egg yolk. Stir in the scallops, tomato purée and cream, then season with salt and pepper. Cook, uncovered, for 2 minutes.

4 Sieve the potatoes and beat together with the remaining butter and milk. Season with salt and pepper. Put the creamed potato in a piping bag fitted with a large star nozzle.

5 Pipe the potato around the edges of 4 scallop shells and spoon the scallop mixture into the centre of each shell. Cook for 2 minutes. Garnish.

SCAMPI SPECIAL

SERVES ▶ 4	
SETTING ▶ HIGH	
TIME ▶ 12 MINUTES	
GRADING ▶ LESS EASY	

45 ml (3 tbsp) olive oil

1 medium onion, skinned and chopped

2 garlic cloves, skinned and crushed

60 ml (4 level tbsp) tomato purée

5 ml (1 tsp) chopped fresh tarragon

300 ml (½ pint) hot fish stock

salt and pepper

450 g (1 lb) prepared scampi

boiled rice, to serve (see page 86)

chopped fresh tarragon, to garnish

1 Put the olive oil, onion and garlic in a 2.75 litre (4½–5 pint) bowl. Cover with cling film, pulling back one corner to allow steam to escape and cook for 5 minutes or until onion is tender. Stir halfway through cooking.

2 Stir in the tomato purée, tarragon, hot stock, salt, pepper and scampi. Re-cover and cook for 7 minutes or until hot. Stir halfway through cooking.

3 Spoon the mixture onto a bed of rice on a warmed serving dish. Garnish with chopped tarragon.

Opposite
Fish Kebabs (page 43)

COD WITH SWEETCORN PURÉE

SERVES ▶	4
SETTING ▶	HIGH
TIME ▶	$9\frac{3}{4}$ MINUTES
GRADING ▶	LESS EASY

4 cod steaks, 175 g (6 oz) each, skinned

75 g (3 oz) butter or margarine, cut into pieces

350 g (12 oz) can sweetcorn, drained

salt and pepper

10 ml (2 tsp) double cream or milk

slices of tomato and mustard and cress, to garnish

1 Place the fish in a shallow dish with the thinner parts towards the centre. Cover with cling film, pulling back one corner to allow steam to escape and cook for 5 minutes. Re-position halfway through cooking. Set aside, covered, while making up the remaining ingredients.

2 Put the butter in a 600 ml (1 pint) jug. Cook, uncovered, for 45 seconds or until melted. Blend the sweetcorn, salt, pepper, cream and melted butter in a blender or food processor.

3 Arrange the cod in a warmed ovenproof serving dish. Spoon the sweetcorn purée over the cod. Cook, uncovered, for 4 minutes or until hot. Garnish with slices of tomato and mustard and cress.

Opposite
Scallops with Tomato Sauce (page 48)

BRILL CREOLE STYLE

SERVES ▶	4
SETTING ▶	HIGH
TIME ▶	11 MINUTES
GRADING ▶	LESS EASY

1 kg (2$\frac{1}{4}$ lb) brill, skinned and filleted

30 ml (2 tbsp) olive oil

2 garlic cloves, skinned and crushed

4 spring onions, trimmed and sliced

$\frac{1}{2}$ red pepper, cored, seeded and diced

$\frac{1}{2}$ green pepper, cored, seeded and diced

4 anchovy fillets, drained and chopped

5 ml (1 tsp) chopped fresh thyme or 1.25 ml ($\frac{1}{4}$ level tsp) dried

2 tomatoes, skinned and chopped

15 ml (1 level tbsp) tomato purée

15 ml (1 level tbsp) white wine

salt and pepper

1 Cut the brill to give four fillets. Roll up each fillet and secure with a wooden cocktail stick. Set aside.

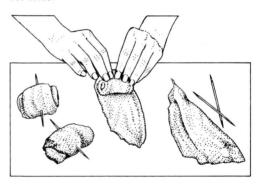

2 Put the oil, garlic, onions, peppers, anchovies, thyme, tomatoes, tomato purée, wine, salt and pepper in a casserole dish. Cover with cling film, pulling back one corner to allow steam to escape and cook for 5 minutes.

3 Arrange the brill around the outside of the casserole and baste with some of the sauce. Re-cover and cook for 6 minutes. Baste halfway through cooking. Stand, covered, for 3 minutes.

4 Arrange the brill on a warmed serving dish. Remove the cocktail sticks. Spoon the vegetables and sauce over the brill.

SEAFOOD MAYONNAISE

SERVES ▶ 4	
SETTING ▶ HIGH	
TIME ▶ 6 MINUTES	
GRADING ▶ LESS EASY	

450 g (1 lb) cod or similar white fish, skinned

75 g (3 oz) cooked prawns, peeled

75 g (3 oz) cooked mussels

75 g (3 oz) cooked cockles

1 small cabbage lettuce, washed, dried and torn into small strips

1 egg yolk

salt and pepper

1.25 ml ($\frac{1}{4}$ level tsp) mustard powder

150–300 ml ($\frac{1}{4}$–$\frac{1}{2}$ pint) olive oil

10 ml (2 tsp) tarragon vinegar

10 ml (2 tsp) wine vinegar

6 anchovy fillets, drained, 4 stuffed olives, sliced, 2 gherkins, cut into tassels, and 8 capers, drained, to garnish

1 Place the cod in a shallow container with the thinner parts towards the centre. Cover with cling film, pulling back one corner to allow steam to escape and cook for 6 minutes. Re-position halfway through cooking. Set aside, covered, until cool.

2 Flake the fish, removing any bones. Cool completely. Gently mix the flaked fish with the prawns, mussels and cockles.

3 Arrange the lettuce on a serving dish and pile the fish mixture in the centre.

4 Put the yolk in a small bowl and whisk in the salt, pepper and mustard. Add the oil very slowly from a teaspoon, beating constantly. When half the oil has been added and the mixture is thick and creamy, add small quantities of vinegar to prevent the sauce getting too thick. After all the vinegar has been added the oil may be added more quickly.

5 Spoon the mayonnaise over the fish. Garnish with a lattice of strips of anchovy, olives, gherkins and capers. Serve immediately.

JELLIED EELS

SERVES ▶ 4
SETTING ▶ HIGH and DEFROST
TIME ▶ 33 MINUTES
GRADING ▶ LESS EASY

1 large onion, skinned and sliced

900 g (2 lb) eels, cleaned, skinned and cut into 5 cm (2 inch) lengths

15 ml (1 tbsp) wine vinegar

2 bay leaves

60 ml (4 tbsp) chopped fresh parsley

5 ml (1 level tsp) allspice

salt and pepper

450 ml ($\frac{3}{4}$ pint) boiling fish stock

parsley sprigs, to garnish

1 Put the onion in a 2.75 litre ($4\frac{1}{2}$–5 pint) bowl. Cover with cling film, pulling back one corner to allow steam to escape and cook on High for 3 minutes or until tender. Stir in the eels, vinegar, bay leaves, parsley, allspice, salt, pepper and boiling fish stock. Re-cover and cook on High for 10 minutes. Stir halfway through cooking.

2 Stir, reduce to Defrost. Cover with cling film, pulling back one corner to allow steam to escape and cook for 20 minutes. Stir halfway through cooking. Pour into a serving bowl. Chill. Garnish with parsley sprigs.

PIQUANT PLAICE

SERVES ▶ 2–4
SETTING ▶ HIGH
TIME ▶ 11 MINUTES
GRADING ▶ LESS EASY

1 medium onion, skinned and chopped

25 g (1 oz) butter or margarine

30 ml (2 level tbsp) tomato purée

2 medium tomatoes, skinned and chopped

100 g (4 oz) mushrooms, sliced

150 ml ($\frac{1}{4}$ pint) hot fish stock

1.25 ml ($\frac{1}{4}$ tsp) ground mace

5 ml (1 level tsp) anchovy essence

salt and pepper

450 g (1 lb) plaice fillets, skinned and cut into strips

chopped fresh parsley, to garnish

1 Put the onion and butter in a 2 litre (3$\frac{1}{2}$ pint) bowl. Cover with cling film, pulling back one corner to allow steam to escape and cook for 5 minutes or until the onion is tender. Stir halfway through cooking.

2 Stir in the tomato purée, tomatoes, mushrooms, stock, mace, anchovy essence, salt and pepper. Re-cover and cook for 2 minutes.

3 Stir in the plaice. Re-cover and cook for 4 minutes. Ladle into a warm serving dish. Garnish with chopped parsley. Serve with boiled rice or creamed potatoes, if wished.

HALIBUT STEAKS WITH PARSLEY SAUCE

SERVES ▶ 4
SETTING ▶ HIGH
TIME ▶ 13 MINUTES
GRADING ▶ LESS EASY

4 halibut steaks, 175 g (6 oz) each, skinned

50 g (2 oz) butter

25 g (1 oz) plain flour

300 ml ($\frac{1}{2}$ pint) milk

2.5 ml ($\frac{1}{2}$ level tsp) Dijon mustard

15 ml (1 tbsp) chopped fresh parsley

salt and pepper

15 ml (1 tbsp) double cream

parsley sprigs, to garnish

1 Place the halibut steaks with the thin ends facing the centre in a shallow dish. Cover with cling film, pulling back one corner to allow steam to escape and cook for 7$\frac{1}{2}$ minutes. Halfway through cooking re-position, if necessary, and dot with 25 g (1 oz) of the butter. Set aside, covered, while making the sauce.

2 Put the remaining butter in a 1 litre (1$\frac{3}{4}$ pint) jug. Cook, uncovered, for 1 minute until melted. Blend in the flour. Cook, uncovered, for 30 seconds. Gradually stir in the milk, mustard, parsley, salt and pepper.

3 Cook, uncovered, for 4 minutes or until thick, stir every minute to avoid lumps. Stir in the liquid from the fish and the cream.

4 Arrange the fish on a warmed serving dish. Coat with the sauce. Garnish with sprigs of fresh parsley.

WHITE FISH STEAKS WITH TARTARE SAUCE

SERVES ▶ 4	
SETTING ▶ HIGH	
TIME ▶ 6 MINUTES	
GRADING ▶ EASY	

150 ml ($\frac{1}{4}$ pint) mayonnaise

10 ml (2 level tsp) finely chopped gherkins

10 ml (2 level tsp) finely chopped capers

10 ml (2 tsp) finely chopped fresh parsley

2.5 ml ($\frac{1}{2}$ tsp) finely chopped fresh tarragon

2.5 ml ($\frac{1}{2}$ tsp) finely chopped fresh chervil

4 cod or halibut steaks, 175 g (6 oz) each, skinned

25 g (1 oz) butter or margarine, cut into 4 pieces

4 gherkins, cut into fans, to garnish

1 Mix together the mayonnaise, gherkins, capers, parsley, tarragon and chervil. Set aside.

2 Place the fish in a shallow dish with the thin ends facing the centre. Cover with cling film, pulling back one corner to allow steam to escape and cook for 4 minutes. Put a piece of butter on each steak. Re-cover and cook for 2 minutes. Stand covered for 5 minutes.

3 Arrange the fish in a warmed serving dish. Just before serving, spoon the mayonnaise over each steak. Garnish with gherkin fans.

SKATE WITH MUSHROOMS

SERVES ▶ 4	
SETTING ▶ HIGH	
TIME ▶ 11 MINUTES	
GRADING ▶ EASY	

2 skate wings, 550 g (1$\frac{1}{4}$ lb) each, skinned

100 g (4 oz) button mushrooms, sliced

75 g (3 oz) butter or margarine, cut into pieces

15 ml (1 tbsp) soured cream

salt and pepper

lemon slices and chopped fresh parsley, to garnish

1 Cut the skate wings in half. Arrange the skate in a 2.75 litre (4$\frac{1}{2}$–5 pint) bowl with the thinner ends facing towards the centre. Cover with cling film, pulling back one corner to allow steam to escape and cook for 5 minutes.

2 Re-position the skate. Cover with the mushrooms and dot with the butter. Re-cover and cook for 5 minutes.

3 Remove the skate and place on a warmed serving dish. In a 600 ml (1 pint) jug, stir the cream into the melted butter and add salt and pepper. Cook, uncovered, for 1 minute or until thickened slightly. Stir after 30 seconds. Pour the butter mixture over the skate. Garnish with lemon slices and parsley.

HOT CRAB WITH FENNEL

SERVES ▶	4
SETTING ▶	HIGH
TIME ▶	10 MINUTES
GRADING ▶	EASY

two 900 g (2 lb) crabs, cooked

100 g (4 oz) butter or margarine, cut into pieces

50 g (2 oz) fennel bulb, finely chopped

4 garlic cloves, skinned and crushed

100 g (4 oz) fresh white breadcrumbs

90 ml (6 tbsp) double cream

salt and pepper

2 hard-boiled eggs, whites and yolks sieved separately and fennel sprigs, to garnish

1 Twist the claws and legs off the crab and crack the shells with a heavy weight. If using the shells as serving dishes, try to crack the shells neatly. Using a skewer, scrape out all the white meat. Place the crabs on their backs and carefully pull the body in the centre away from the shell. Remove and discard the greyish white stomach sac and the grey feathered gills. Using a fork, scrape out the meat and mix with the white meat. Scrub the shells clean and set aside.

2 Put the butter, fennel and garlic in a 2.75 litre (4½–5 pint) bowl. Cover with cling film, pulling back one corner to allow steam to escape and cook for 3 minutes or until the fennel is tender. Stir in the breadcrumbs, crab flesh, cream, salt and pepper. Re-cover and cook for 7 minutes or until hot. Stir halfway through cooking.

3 Spoon the mixture into the scrubbed crab shells.

4 Garnish with sieved egg yolk and white and fennel sprigs.

PRAWN CURRY

SERVES ▶	4
SETTING ▶	HIGH
TIME ▶	20 MINUTES
GRADING ▶	EASY

50 g (2 oz) butter or margarine

1 large onion, skinned and finely chopped

1 garlic clove, skinned and crushed

15 ml (1 level tbsp) plain flour

10 ml (2 level tsp) turmeric

2.5 ml (½ level tsp) ground cloves

5 ml (1 level tsp) ground cinnamon

5 ml (1 level tsp) salt

5 ml (1 level tsp) sugar

50 g (2 oz) creamed coconut

450 ml (¾ pint) hot chicken stock

450 g (1 lb) peeled prawns

5 ml (1 tsp) lemon juice

1 Put the butter in a 2 litre (3½ pint) bowl and cook uncovered for 45 seconds or until melted. Stir in the onion and garlic. Cover with cling film, pulling back one corner to allow steam to escape and cook for 7 minutes, or until the onions are tender.

2 Stir in the flour, spices, salt and sugar and cook uncovered for 2 minutes. Stir in the creamed coconut and stock and cook for 6–8 minutes until boiling. Stir halfway through cooking.

3 Add the prawns and lemon juice and cook uncovered for 1–2 minutes until the prawns are heated through.

POULTRY

MICROWAVE COURSE GUIDANCE

Always ensure poultry is completely thawed before cooking.

Poultry may be roasted covered in cling film with one corner pulled back to allow steam to escape, in a bag or open roasted. If a roasting bag is used, pierce it in several places to allow steam to escape and tie with a non-metallic tie.

When cooking small pieces of poultry, such as chicken legs, try to arrange them with the thinner parts towards the centre of the container.

The thinner parts of poultry can be carefully covered with small amounts of foil to avoid overcooking.

Whole birds must be left to stand after microwave cooking.

When roasting whole poultry, using a trivet keeps the juices from the underside of the bird.

Fatty poultry, such as duck and goose, should have the juices poured off during the cooking process.

If using a thermometer, ensure that it does not touch any bone but is inserted into the thickest part of the meat, e.g. the thigh.

If wished birds may be glazed halfway through the cooking with a mixture of
30 ml (2 tbsp) honey
5 ml (1 tsp) Worcestershire sauce
5 ml (1 tsp) soy sauce

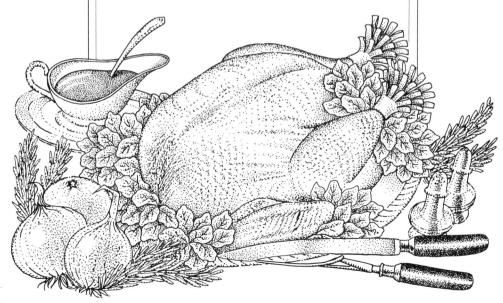

BASIC ROAST

CHICKEN

SERVES ▶ 4	
SETTING ▶ HIGH	
TIME ▶ 28 MINUTES	
GRADING ▶ EASY	

1.8 kg (4 lb) roasting chicken

1 Truss the chicken. If necessary, wrap foil around the thinner parts, such as the wing tips. Place the bird, breast side down, on a trivet in a shallow dish. Cook, uncovered, for 28 minutes. Turn over halfway through cooking. Remove the foil shields at the end of the cooking time.

2 Either: wrap the bird tightly in foil for 15 minutes before carving. Or: remove the bird from the microwave cooker and place it in a conventional oven, preheated to 190°C (375°F) mark 5, for 15–20 minutes, until brown.

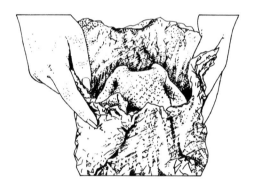

3 Serve with roast potatoes, vegetables, sausages, bacon rolls and bread sauce, if wished.

─────── TIPS ───────

ALLOW 7 MINUTES PER 450 g (1 lb) WHEN COOKING CHICKEN.

IF THE CHICKEN IS STUFFED ALLOW A FURTHER 1 MINUTE PER 450 g (1 lb).

BASIC ROAST

TURKEY

SERVES ▶ 6–8	
SETTING ▶ HIGH	
TIME ▶ 53 MINUTES	
GRADING ▶ EASY	

3.2 kg (7 lb) turkey

1 Truss the turkey. If necessary, wrap small pieces of foil around the thinner parts, such as the wing tips. Place, breast side down, on a trivet in a shallow dish. Cover with absorbent kitchen paper. Cook for 26 minutes.

2 Remove the foil pieces from the turkey. Drain off the juices. Discard the absorbent kitchen paper.

3 Replace the bird on the trivet, breast side up. Cook for a further 27 minutes.

4 Either: wrap the turkey tightly in foil and allow it to stand for 30 minutes. Or: remove the turkey from the microwave cooker and place it in a conventional oven, preheated to 190°C (375°F) mark 5 for 30 minutes or until it is crisp and brown.

5 Serve with roast potatoes, vegetables, sausage meatballs and cranberry sauce, if wished.

─────── TIPS ───────

ALLOW 7½ MINUTES PER 450 g (1 lb) WHEN COOKING TURKEYS UP TO 4.5 kg (10 lb).

IF THE COOKER HAS A TURNTABLE CHECK THAT IT IS ABLE TO TURN FREELY THROUGHOUT THE COOKING OF A TURKEY. ALSO IF FOIL IS USED CHECK CAREFULLY THAT THE FOIL DOES NOT TOUCH THE COOKING CAVITY WALLS.

FOIL CAN BE SECURED WITH WOODEN COCKTAIL STICKS.

BASIC ROAST DUCK

SERVES ▶	4
SETTING ▶	HIGH
TIME ▶	40 MINUTES
GRADING ▶	EASY

2.7 kg (6 lb) duck

1 Truss the duck and prick all over so the fat can escape. If necessary, wrap small pieces of foil around the thinner parts such as the wing tips. Place in a roasting bag and secure with a non-metallic tie. Prick the bag.

2 Place the bird, breast side down, on a trivet in a shallow dish. Cook for 20 minutes. Remove the bag and carefully drain off juices.

3 Replace the duck on the trivet, breast side up. Cook, uncovered, for a further 20 minutes.

4 Either: wrap the duck tightly in foil for 15 minutes, then brown under a preheated grill if a crispy skin is desired. Or: remove the bird from the microwave and place in a conventional oven, preheated to 200°C (400°F) mark 6, for 15 minutes or until crisp and brown.

5 Serve with roast potatoes, a green vegetable and apple sauce, if wished.

——— TIPS ———

ALLOW 6½ MINUTES PER 450 g (1 lb) WHEN COOKING A DUCK.

IF THE DUCK IS STUFFED ALLOW AN EXTRA 1 MINUTE PER 450 g (1 lb).

TO GIVE AN ORANGE FLAVOUR, CUT UP AN ORANGE AND INSERT THE PIECES IN THE CAVITY OF THE DUCK BEFORE COOKING.

TURKEY LIVERS COOKED IN ORANGE

SERVES ▶	4
SETTING ▶	HIGH
TIME ▶	14 MINUTES
GRADING ▶	EASY

100 g (4 oz) butter or margarine

2 garlic cloves, skinned and crushed

30 ml (2 level tbsp) tomato purée

10 ml (2 tsp) chopped fresh basil or 5 ml (1 level tsp) dried

800 g (1¾ lb) turkey livers, chopped

2 small oranges, peeled, seeded, segmented and segments cut in half

25 g (1 oz) cornflour

150 ml (¼ pint) fresh orange juice

45 ml (3 tbsp) dry sherry

salt and pepper

30 ml (2 tbsp) soured cream

chopped fresh parsley and orange slices, to garnish

boiled rice, to serve (see page 86)

1 Put the butter, garlic, tomato purée and basil in a 2.75 litre (4½–5 pint) bowl. Cover with cling film, pulling back one corner to allow steam to escape and cook for 2 minutes.

2 Stir in the livers. Re-cover and cook for 4 minutes, then stir in the orange segments. Continue cooking for a further 2 minutes.

3 Blend together the cornflour, orange juice and sherry. Stir into the livers. Season with salt and pepper. Cover with cling film again, leaving the corner turned back, and cook for 6 minutes or until tender. Stir halfway through cooking.

4 Swirl the soured cream into the sauce and the livers. Arrange in a warmed serving dish. Garnish with chopped parsley and orange slices and serve with boiled rice.

TURKEY BREASTS WITH WHISKY SAUCE

SERVES ▶ 4
SETTING ▶ HIGH and using a conventional hob
TIME ▶ 8½ MINUTES
GRADING ▶ LESS EASY

4 turkey fillets, from the breast, 100 g (4 oz) each

75 g (3 oz) butter or margarine

2 large oranges, rind removed with a zester, pith removed and the oranges sliced

10 ml (2 level tsp) cornflour

90 ml (6 tbsp) orange juice

60 ml (4 tbsp) whisky

10 ml (2 level tsp) soft dark brown sugar

salt and pepper

watercress, to garnish

1 Roll up the turkey fillets and secure them with wooden cocktail sticks. Place in a shallow dish. Cover with cling film, pulling back one corner to allow steam to escape and cook for 5 minutes. Halfway through cooking re-position and turn over.

2 Put 25 g (1 oz) of the butter in a frying pan and heat on a conventional hob. Remove the cocktail sticks from the fillets. Fry the fillets in the butter until golden brown. Set aside to keep warm. Add the sliced oranges to the pan and fry until soft.

3 Meanwhile, blend the cornflour and orange juice in a 1 litre (1¾ pint) jug. Stir in the whisky, sugar, orange rind, remaining butter, salt and pepper. Cook, uncovered, for 3½ minutes, stirring every minute until hot and thickened.

4 Arrange the orange slices on a warmed serving dish. Place the fillets on top and spoon the sauce over them. Garnish with watercress. Serve with creamed potatoes and French beans if wished.

ROAST GOOSE WITH NUT STUFFING

SERVES ▶ 6–8
SETTING ▶ HIGH and using a conventional oven
TIME ▶ 41 MINUTES
GRADING ▶ LESS EASY

25 g (1 oz) butter or margarine

1 medium onion, skinned and finely chopped

100 g (4 oz) fresh brown breadcrumbs

150 ml (¼ pint) hot chicken stock

15 ml (1 tbsp) chopped fresh tarragon or 5 ml (1 level tsp) dried

15 ml (1 tbsp) chopped fresh rosemary or 5 ml (1 level tsp) dried

1 dessert apple, peeled, cored and chopped

30 ml (2 level tbsp) chopped mixed nuts

salt and pepper

2.7 kg (6 lb) goose, prepared weight, thawed, if frozen

watercress sprigs, to garnish

1 Put the butter and onion in a 2 litre (3½ pint) bowl. Cover with cling film, pulling back one corner to allow steam to escape and cook for 5 minutes. Stir in the breadcrumbs, stock, tarragon, rosemary, apple, nuts, salt and pepper.

2 Use the mixture to stuff the neck end of the goose and secure the opening with wooden cocktail sticks. Mask the wings and thin ends of the legs with small pieces of foil. Truss the bird with string.

3 Place the goose, breast side down, on a trivet in a shallow container. Cover with absorbent kitchen paper. Cook for 18 minutes.

4 Turn the bird over and drain off the excess fat. Remove the small pieces of masking foil. Cover the bird with fresh absorbent kitchen paper. Cook for a further 18 minutes.

5 Wrap the goose tightly in foil and allow it to stand for 20 minutes. Remove the wooden cocktail sticks and place the bird on a warmed serving dish. Garnish with sprigs of watercress.

GARLIC CHICKEN PARCELS

SERVES ▶ 4	
SETTING ▶ HIGH	
TIME ▶ 11 MINUTES	
GRADING ▶ LESS EASY	

4 chicken breast fillets, 100 g (4 oz) each, skinned

40 g (1½ oz) butter or margarine

2 garlic cloves, skinned and chopped or crushed

10 ml (2 tsp) chopped fresh tarragon or 2.5 ml (½ level tsp) dried

4 rashers back bacon, rinded

tarragon sprigs, to garnish

1 Beat the breasts to flatten them. Cream together the butter, garlic and tarragon. Divide and spread the mixture over each chicken breast. Roll up the breasts with the butter inside.

2 Using the back of a knife, stretch each rasher of bacon. Roll a rasher of bacon around each chicken fillet. If necessary, secure with wooden cocktail sticks.

3 Arrange the parcels in a circle on an ovenproof pie plate. Cover with cling film, and pull back one corner to allow steam to escape, then cook for 11 minutes. Re-position halfway through cooking. Stand, covered, for 2 minutes before serving. Remove the wooden cocktail sticks, if used.

4 Place the parcels on a warmed serving dish. Spoon over the cooking juices. Garnish each parcel with tarragon sprigs. Serve with creamed potatoes and broccoli, if wished.

SWEET AND SOUR DUCK

SERVES ▶ 4	
SETTING ▶ HIGH and using a conventional hob	
TIME ▶ 22½ MINUTES	
GRADING ▶ LESS EASY	

1 medium onion, skinned and chopped

1 garlic clove, skinned and crushed

½ green pepper, cored, seeded and diced

25 g (1 oz) butter or margarine

25 g (1 oz) plain flour

300 ml (½ pint) hot chicken stock

30 ml (2 tbsp) malt vinegar

15 ml (1 tbsp) soy sauce

15 ml (1 level tbsp) blackcurrant jam

100 g (4 oz) raisins

50 g (2 oz) soft dark brown sugar

4 duck breast fillets, each weighing 175 g (6 oz)

vegetable oil, for conventional frying

1 Put the onion, garlic, pepper and butter in a 1 litre (1¾ pint) jug. Cover with cling film, pulling back one corner to allow steam to escape and cook for 6 minutes or until the onion is tender. Stir halfway through cooking.

2 Stir in the flour and cook, uncovered, for 30 seconds. Gradually blend in the stock. Stir in the vinegar, soy sauce, blackcurrant jam, raisins and brown sugar. Cook, uncovered, for 3 minutes. Stir every minute. Set aside while cooking the duck.

3 Arrange the breast fillets over the base of a shallow dish. Cover with cling film, pulling back one corner to allow steam to escape and cook for 10 minutes. Re-position and turn over halfway through cooking, pour off any juices into a jug and reserve.

4 Heat a little oil in a frying pan and fry the duck fillets on a conventional hob until crisp and brown. Meanwhile, reheat the sauce, uncovered, for 3 minutes or until hot. Stir halfway through cooking.

5 Arrange the duck in a warmed serving dish and pour the hot sauce over.

DUCK TERRINE

SERVES ▶ 4	
SETTING ▶ HIGH	
TIME ▶ 5–6 MINUTES	
GRADING ▶ LESS EASY	

50 g (2 oz) mushrooms, finely chopped

275 g (10 oz) cooked boned duck, chopped

1 garlic clove, skinned and crushed

*15 ml (1 tbsp) chopped fresh mixed herbs or
  5 ml (1 level tsp) dried*

salt and pepper

2 eggs, lightly beaten

*sliced tomatoes and sliced hard-boiled eggs, to
  garnish*

1 Mix together the mushrooms, duck, garlic, herbs, salt and pepper. Bind with the eggs.

2 Grease and base-line a 16 cm (6½ inch) soufflé dish with greaseproof paper. Place an inverted glass tumbler in the centre.

3 Spoon and spread the mixture evenly around the dish and the glass.

4 Cover with cling film, pulling back one corner to allow steam to escape and cook for 5–6 minutes. Turn out the terrine on to a warmed serving dish. Garnish with slices of tomato and slices of hard-boiled eggs. Serve hot or cold with a mixed green salad, if wished.

——— TIP ———

USE ANY OTHER COOKED POULTRY, IF PREFERRED.

RABBIT CASSEROLE

SERVES ▶ 4	
SETTING ▶ HIGH and DEFROST	
TIME ▶ 59½ MINUTES	
GRADING ▶ LESS EASY	

8 rabbit joints, 100 g (4 oz) each

225 g (8 oz) carrots, peeled and sliced

1 medium onion, skinned and chopped

1.25 ml (¼ level tsp) ground mace

5 ml (1 level tsp) dried thyme

25 g (1 oz) butter or margarine

25 g (1 oz) plain flour

100 ml (4 fl oz) milk

450 ml (¾ pint) hot chicken stock

salt and pepper

1 Place the rabbit joints around a 2.75 litre (4½–5 pint) bowl with the thinnest ends towards the centre of the bowl. Cover the bowl with cling film, pulling back one corner to allow steam to escape and cook for 10 minutes. Re-position halfway through cooking. Remove the joints and set aside.

2 Add the carrots, onion, mace, thyme and butter to the rabbit liquid in the bowl. Re-cover and cook for 8 minutes. Stir halfway through the cooking

3 Stir in the flour and cook, uncovered, for 30 seconds. Gradually add the milk, stock, salt and pepper. Cook, uncovered, for 3 minutes. Stir every minute.

4 Prick the rabbit joints and add to the sauce, flesh side down. Add any liquid from the rabbit. Cook, covered with cling film as before, for 8 minutes. Stir halfway through cooking.

5 Reduce to Defrost. Cook for 30 minutes or until tender. Serve with creamed potatoes, if wished.

——— TIP ———

IF PREFERRED, USE CHICKEN JOINTS FOR THIS RECIPE.

MEAT

MICROWAVE COURSE GUIDANCE

Always ensure joints of meat are completely thawed before cooking.

Joints may be roasted covered, in a bag or open roasted. If covered using roasting bags, tie them with a non-metallic tie and pierce the bag to allow the steam to escape.

Regularly shaped joints are easier to cook, but if, for example, a leg of lamb is being roasted, then shield the thin end with a small piece of foil.

Joints must be left to stand after cooking. They can be wrapped in foil or put in a conventional oven to brown for 15–20 minutes.

Small cuts of meat such as steaks and chops can have improved colour if microwave browning agents are used. For those who prefer a crispy finish, the speed of microwave cooking can be used, then the browning of the food can be achieved by grilling or frying on the conventional hob.

If the Defrost position is used for the slow cooking of tougher meat, always ensure that the initial cooking is carried out on High for about 10 minutes or until meat has been thoroughly heated through.

When roasting meat, using a trivet keeps the juices from the underside of the meat and helps the meat to brown.

If using a meat thermometer, ensure that it does not touch the bone in the meat but is inserted into the thickest part of the joint.

HEATING CANNED MEAT

SERVES ▶ 2
SETTING ▶ HIGH
TIME ▶ 5 MINUTES
GRADING ▶ VERY EASY

411 g (14½ oz) can braised beef

Put the meat and gravy in a 1.2 litre (2 pint) bowl. Cover with cling film, pulling back one corner to allow steam to escape and cook for 5 minutes or until hot. Stir halfway through cooking. Serve with potatoes and cabbage, if wished.

———— TIP ————

FOR A QUICK MEAT AND VEGETABLE STEW, ADD A SMALL CAN OF MIXED VEGETABLES BUT INCREASE THE COOKING TIME BY 3–4 MINUTES.

ROASTING BEEF, LAMB, PORK OR VEAL JOINTS

SERVES ▶ 4–6
SETTING ▶ HIGH
TIME ▶ Depends on the size and joint of meat
GRADING ▶ EASY

Joint of meat 1.4 kg (3 lb) or over

1 Place the joint on a trivet in a shallow container. Cook, uncovered, or in a roasting bag. Allow:

Beef	rare	5 minutes per 450 g (1 lb)
	medium	6–7 minutes per 450 g (1 lb)
	well done	8–9 minutes per 450 g (1 lb)
Lamb		7–8 minutes per 450 g (1 lb)
Pork		9 minutes per 450 g (1 lb)
Veal		9 minutes per 450 g (1 lb)

2 Pour off the juices and keep them for the gravy. Transfer the meat to a conventional oven, preheated to 190°C (375°F) mark 5, for 15–20 minutes or until the meat is browned sufficiently.

3 Alternatively, after taking the meat out of the microwave cooker, remove the roasting bag if used, and wrap the meat tightly in foil. Allow it to stand for 15–20 minutes before carving.

———— TIP ————

TO CRISP CRACKLING ON THE PORK, REMOVE THE FAT FROM THE MEAT AND PLACE IT UNDER A PREHEATED GRILL. IF FINISHING THE JOINT IN A CONVENTIONAL OVEN, RUB THE SKIN WITH VEGETABLE OIL AND SALT BEFORE PLACING IT IN THE OVEN.

BASIC MINCE

SERVES ▶ 4
SETTING ▶ HIGH
TIME ▶ 10 MINUTES
GRADING ▶ EASY

1 medium onion, skinned and chopped

450 g (1 lb) minced meat

2.5 ml (½ level tsp) dried mixed herbs

1 beef stock cube, crumbled

15 ml (1 level tbsp) tomato purée

salt and pepper

1 Put the onion in a 2 litre (3½ pint) bowl. Cover with cling film, pulling back one corner to allow steam to escape and cook for 5 minutes or until the onion is tender.

2 Stir in the meat, herbs, stock cube, tomato purée, salt and pepper. Re-cover and cook for 5 minutes or until cooked. Stir halfway through cooking. Serve with creamed potatoes and peas or swede, if wished.

——— TIPS ———

USE TOMATO SAUCE INSTEAD OF TOMATO PURÉE IF PREFERRED.

ADD A SMALL CAN OF BAKED BEANS TO THE MINCE TO MAKE A MORE FILLING RECIPE.

COVER THE MINCE WITH INSTANT MASHED POTATOES AND BROWN UNDER THE GRILL TO MAKE A QUICK SHEPHERD'S PIE.

BACON AND ONION PUDDING

SERVES ▶ 4
SETTING ▶ HIGH
TIME ▶ 14 MINUTES
GRADING ▶ EASY

1 large onion, skinned and finely chopped

8 rashers bacon, rinded and chopped

salt and pepper

15 ml (1 tbsp) chopped fresh sage or 5 ml (1 level tsp) dried

225 g (8 oz) self-raising flour

100 g (4 oz) shredded suet

1 egg, size 2, lightly beaten with 30 ml (2 tbsp) water

1 Place the onion in a 2 litre (3½ pint) bowl. Cover with cling film, pulling back one corner to allow steam to escape and cook for 7 minutes. Stir halfway through cooking.

2 Stir in the bacon, salt, pepper, sage, flour and suet. Mix the egg into the dry ingredients. Put in a greased 1.4 litre (2½ pint) basin. Cook, covered with cling film as before, for 7 minutes or until the centre is cooked.

3 Stand, covered, for 2 minutes. Remove the cover and loosen the edges of the pudding with a knife. Turn out on to a warmed serving dish. Serve with creamed potatoes and cabbage or carrots, if wished.

——— TIP ———

THIS PUDDING SHOULD BE SERVED FRESHLY MADE. IT TENDS TO HARDEN ON COOLING.

ROAST LAMB WITH HONEY

SERVES ▶	4–6
SETTING ▶	HIGH and using a conventional oven
TIME ▶	40–45 MINUTES
GRADING ▶	EASY

1.6 kg (3½ lb) leg of lamb

45 ml (3 tbsp) clear honey

chopped fresh mint or parsley, to garnish

1 Wrap the thin end of the leg in a small band of foil. Using a metal skewer prick the joint. Brush the joint with 15 ml (1 tbsp) of the honey.

2 Place on a trivet in a shallow ovenproof container. Cook, uncovered, for 25 minutes. After 15 minutes, brush with a further 15 ml (1 tbsp) of honey and remove the foil band.

3 Pour off the juices and set aside for the gravy. Transfer the meat to a conventional oven, preheated to 190°C (375°F) mark 5. Brush with the remaining honey. Cook for 15–20 minutes. Garnish the meat with a generous sprinkling of chopped fresh mint or parsley. Serve with roast potatoes, carrots and peas, if wished.

——— TIP ———

IF PREFERRED, AFTER REMOVING THE LAMB FROM THE MICROWAVE COOKER IT CAN BE BRUSHED WITH THE REMAINING HONEY, THEN WRAPPED TIGHTLY IN FOIL AND LEFT TO STAND FOR 20 MINUTES BEFORE SERVING.

SWEET AND SOUR SPARE RIBS

SERVES ▶	4
SETTING ▶	HIGH
TIME ▶	28 MINUTES
GRADING ▶	EASY

1 medium onion, skinned and chopped

½ green pepper, cored, seeded and diced

½ red pepper, cored, seeded and diced

7.5 ml (1½ level tsp) mixed dried herbs

1 garlic clove, skinned and crushed

25 g (1 oz) butter or margarine

25 g (1 oz) plain flour

30 ml (2 tbsp) white wine vinegar

15 ml (1 tbsp) soy sauce

300 ml (½ pint) hot chicken stock

50 g (2 oz) soft dark brown sugar

700 g (1½ lb) pork spare ribs, separated

1 Put the onion, peppers, herbs, garlic and butter in a 2.75 litre (4½–5 pint) bowl. Cover with cling film, pulling back one corner to allow steam to escape and cook for 6½ minutes or until the vegetables are tender. Stir halfway through cooking.

2 Stir in the flour and cook, uncovered, for 30 seconds. Gradually blend in the vinegar, soy sauce, hot chicken stock and brown sugar. Cook, uncovered, for 3 minutes, until boiled and thickened. Stir every minute.

3 Add the ribs and cook, covered with cling film as before, for 18 minutes. Re-position and baste halfway through cooking. Stand, covered, for 5 minutes before serving.

4 Arrange the ribs in a shallow warmed serving dish. Pour the sauce over the ribs. Serve with a mixed green salad, if wished.

CROWN ROAST WITH BLACKBERRY STUFFING

SERVES ▶ 4
SETTING ▶ HIGH
TIME ▶ 32–34 MINUTES
GRADING ▶ LESS EASY

175 g (6 oz) blackberries, thawed if frozen

15 ml (1 level tbsp) caster sugar

1 medium onion, skinned and finely chopped

25 g (1 oz) butter or margarine, cut into pieces

meat trimmings from prepared crown, finely chopped

100 g (4 oz) fresh white breadcrumbs

15 ml (1 tbsp) chopped fresh parsley

15 ml (1 tbsp) chopped fresh thyme or 5 ml (1 level tsp) dried

salt and pepper

1 egg, lightly beaten

1 crown roast lamb, prepared weight 1 kg (2¼ lb), made up of 12–14 chops

1 Put the blackberries and sugar in a 1 litre (1¾ pint) jug. Cook, uncovered, for 3–5 minutes, until soft. Stir halfway through cooking. Sieve to remove the seeds.

2 Put the onion, butter and meat trimmings in a 2 litre (3½ pint) bowl. Cover with cling film, pulling back one corner to allow steam to escape and cook for 4 minutes. Drain off the excess fat and mix the onion mixture together with the sieved blackberries, breadcrumbs, parsley, thyme, salt and pepper. Add sufficient egg to bind the mixture.

3 Place the crown on a dish, stuff the centre then place on a trivet or an upturned dish. Cook, uncovered, for 25 minutes. Turn round halfway through cooking.

4 Wrap the crown tightly in foil and stand for 20 minutes. Place on a warmed serving dish. Garnish with cutlet frills. Serve with boiled potatoes, broccoli or beans if wished.

PORK WITH BLACK GRAPES

SERVES ▶ 4
SETTING ▶ HIGH
TIME ▶ 10¾ MINUTES
GRADING ▶ LESS EASY

8 pork escalopes, 50 g (2 oz) each

25 g (1 oz) butter or margarine

25 g (1 oz) plain flour

150 ml (¼ pint) unsweetened apple juice

150 ml (¼ pint) hot chicken stock

salt and pepper

175 g (6 oz) black grapes, cut in half and seeded

15 ml (1 tbsp) double cream (optional)

vegetable oil, for conventional frying

1 Arrange the escalopes over the base of a shallow ovenproof dish, overlapping if necessary. Cover with cling film, pulling back one corner to allow steam to escape and cook for 6 minutes or until the juices run clear when the escalopes are pricked. After 3 minutes re-position. Set aside, covered.

2 Put the butter in a 1 litre (1¾ pint) jug. Cook, uncovered, for 45 seconds or until melted. Stir in the flour and cook, uncovered, for 30 seconds. Gradually blend in the apple juice and then the stock. Season with salt and pepper. Cook, uncovered, for 2½ minutes or until thick. Stir every minute.

3 Stir the grapes into the sauce. Cook, uncovered, for 1 minute or until hot. Stir in the cream, if using. Check the seasoning.

4 Arrange the escalopes on a warmed serving dish. Pour the sauce over the escalopes. Serve with a mixed green salad, if wished.

Opposite
*R*abbit *C*asserole (page 59)

PORK PAPRIKA

SERVES ▶ 4
SETTING ▶ HIGH and DEFROST
TIME ▶ 57 MINUTES
GRADING ▶ LESS EASY

700 g (1½ lb) pork fillet, cubed

75 g (3 oz) bacon rashers, rinded and chopped

1 large onion, skinned and chopped

100 g (4 oz) button mushrooms

15 ml (1 level tbsp) tomato purée

30 ml (2 level tbsp) paprika

salt and pepper

45 ml (3 tbsp) soured cream

5 ml (1 level tsp) cornflour

chopped fresh parsley, to garnish

boiled rice, to serve (see page 86)

1 Put the pork and bacon in a 2.75 litre (4½–5 pint) bowl. Cover with cling film, pulling back one corner to allow steam to escape and cook for 5 minutes. Stir in the onion, mushrooms, tomato purée, paprika, salt and pepper. Re-cover and cook for 9 minutes or until the onion is tender. Stir halfway through cooking.

2 Stir, reduce to Defrost and continue cooking, covered with cling film as before, for 40 minutes, or until the pork is tender. Stir occasionally.

3 Stir the soured cream into the cornflour, then stir into the meat mixture. Cook, uncovered, for 3 minutes but do not boil. Stir every minute during cooking.

4 Spoon on to a warmed serving dish and garnish with chopped fresh parsley. Serve with boiled rice.

PORK CHOPS WITH GREEN PEPPERS

SERVES ▶ 4
SETTING ▶ HIGH and DEFROST
TIME ▶ 40½ MINUTES
GRADING ▶ LESS EASY

4 pork chops, 150 g (5 oz) each

1 green pepper, cored, seeded and thinly sliced

3 spring onions, chopped

50 g (2 oz) mushrooms, sliced

2.5 ml (½ level tsp) ground coriander

25 g (1 oz) butter or margarine

2 garlic cloves, skinned and crushed

15 ml (1 level tbsp) tomato purée

25 g (1 oz) plain flour

150 ml (¼ pint) vermouth rosé

450 ml (¾ pint) hot chicken stock

salt and pepper

1 Place the chops in the base of a casserole dish. Cover with cling film, pulling back one corner to allow steam to escape and cook for 6 minutes or until tender. Rearrange halfway through cooking. Set aside, covered.

2 In a large bowl, put the pepper, onions, mushrooms, coriander, butter, garlic and tomato purée. Cover with cling film, pulling back one corner to allow steam to escape and cook for 5 minutes.

3 Stir in the flour and cook, uncovered, for 30 seconds. Gradually blend in the vermouth, hot stock, salt and pepper. Cook, covered with cling film as before, for 4 minutes or until thick. Stir every minute.

4 Pour the sauce over the chops. Reduce to Defrost (30%). Re-cover and cook for 25 minutes or until tender. Remove the cling film for the last 10 minutes of cooking time.

5 Arrange the chops on a warmed serving dish. Strain the sauce. Place the vegetables on top of the chops and hand the sauce separately. Serve with sweetcorn and sauté potatoes, if wished.

Opposite
Crown **R**oast with **B**lackberry **S**tuffing (page 64)

VEAL OLIVES

SERVES ▶ 4
SETTING ▶ HIGH and using a conventional grill
TIME ▶ 12¼ MINUTES
GRADING ▶ LESS EASY

50 g (2 oz) cooked ham

1 small onion, skinned and quartered

15 ml (1 tbsp) sweet sherry

30 ml (2 tbsp) hot lamb stock, plus 150 ml (¼ pint)

5 ml (1 tsp) chopped fresh tarragon or 2.5 ml (½ level tsp) dried

50 g (2 oz) mushrooms, roughly chopped

1 garlic clove, skinned and crushed

1 tomato, skinned and quartered

salt and pepper

40–50 g (1½–2 oz) fresh white breadcrumbs

4 veal escalopes, 200 g (7 oz) each, lightly beaten

melted butter, to brush

25 g (1 oz) butter or margarine

25 g (1 oz) plain flour

150 ml (¼ pint) dry white wine

1 Purée the ham, onion, sherry, 30 ml (2 tbsp) of the stock, tarragon, mushrooms, garlic, tomato, salt and pepper, in a blender or food processor. Mix the breadcrumbs into the mixture to make a firm stuffing.

2 Divide the mixture between the veal escalopes and form them into small parcels. Secure with string. Place in a shallow dish. Cover with cling film, pulling back one corner to allow steam to escape and cook for 8 minutes or until tender. Turn over and re-position halfway through cooking. Drain off the juices and set aside. Brush each escalope with a little melted butter and brown under the grill. Or set aside, covered, for 6–10 minutes.

3 Put the butter in a large jug. Cook, uncovered, for 45 seconds or until melted. Stir in the flour and cook, uncovered, for 30 seconds. Gradually stir in the wine, the juices from the meat and the remaining hot stock. Cook, uncovered, for 3 minutes or until thick. Stir every minute. Remove the string from the escalopes and serve.

MINTED LAMB CHOPS

SERVES ▶ 4
SETTING ▶ HIGH and DEFROST
TIME ▶ 36½ MINUTES
GRADING ▶ LESS EASY

1 medium onion, skinned and chopped

1 garlic clove, skinned and crushed

30 ml (2 tbsp) chopped fresh mint

25 g (1 oz) butter or margarine

4 loin lamb chops, 175 g (6 oz) each

100 g (4 oz) mushrooms, chopped

15 g (½ oz) plain flour

150 ml (¼ pint) hot chicken stock

salt and pepper

fresh mint sprigs, to garnish

1 Put the onion, garlic, mint and butter in a 2.75 litre (4½–5 pint) bowl. Cover with cling film, pulling back one corner to allow steam to escape and cook for 5 minutes or until tender.

2 Add the chops and mushrooms. Re-cover and cook for 6 minutes. Remove chops. Stir in the flour and cook, uncovered, for 30 seconds. Gradually blend in the hot stock, salt and pepper. Return the chops to the sauce.

3 Re-cover and cook for 5 minutes. Stir every minute. Re-arrange the chops. Reduce to Defrost for 20 minutes or until tender. Re-arrange and stir halfway through cooking.

4 Place the chops on a warmed serving dish. Pour the liquid and vegetables into a blender or food processor and blend until smooth. Pour the sauce over the chops. Garnish with fresh mint sprigs. Serve with buttered potatoes and peas or runner beans, if wished.

BEEF AND ORANGE CASSEROLE

SERVES ▶ 3
SETTING ▶ HIGH and DEFROST
TIME ▶ 75 MINUTES
GRADING ▶ LESS EASY

1 medium green pepper, cored, seeded and cut into matchsticks

1 medium onion, skinned and finely chopped

grated rind and juice of 2 oranges

25 g (1 oz) butter or margarine

5 ml (1 level tsp) dried rosemary

5 ml (1 level tsp) tomato purée

900 g (2 lb) braising steak, cut into 2.5 cm (1 inch) cubes

15 g ($\frac{1}{2}$ oz) plain flour

150 ml ($\frac{1}{4}$ pint) hot beef stock

salt and pepper

1 small orange, segmented

fresh rosemary sprigs, to garnish

boiled rice (see page 86) or potatoes, to serve

1 Put the pepper, onion, orange rind, butter and rosemary in a 2.75 litre (4$\frac{1}{2}$–5 pint) bowl. Cover with cling film, pulling back one edge to allow steam to escape and cook for 5 minutes. Stir in the tomato purée, steak, flour, orange juice, hot beef stock, salt and pepper. Re-cover and cook for 15 minutes. Stir every 2 minutes during cooking.

2 Reduce to Defrost. Cook, covered with cling film as before, for 50 minutes or until the meat is tender, then stir in the orange segments. Cook, uncovered, for 5 minutes.

3 Transfer to a warmed serving dish. Garnish with rosemary sprigs. Serve with boiled rice or potatoes, if you wish.

STEAK AND MUSHROOM PUDDING

SERVES ▶ 4
SETTING ▶ HIGH and DEFROST
TIME ▶ 72$\frac{1}{2}$ MINUTES
GRADING ▶ LESS EASY

450 g (1 lb) stewing or braising steak, diced

150 ml ($\frac{1}{4}$ pint) red wine

1 medium onion, skinned and chopped

7.5 ml (1$\frac{1}{2}$ level tsp) dried mixed herbs

25 g (1 oz) plain flour

salt and pepper

100 g (4 oz) mushrooms, chopped

225 g (8 oz) self-raising flour

100 g (4 oz) shredded suet

1 Place the steak in a bowl. Pour the wine over the steak. Marinate for 24 hours. Stir several times. Remove the meat and reserve the wine.

2 Put the onion and herbs in a 2.75 litre (4$\frac{1}{2}$–5 pint) bowl. Cover with cling film, pulling back one corner to allow steam to escape and cook for 5 minutes or until the onion is tender. Stir in the meat. Cook for 3 minutes. Stir in the plain flour and cook, uncovered, for 30 seconds. Gradually stir in the reserved wine, salt and pepper. Re-cover and cook for 10 minutes. Stir several times during cooking.

3 Reduce to Defrost. Cook, covered with cling film as before, for 35 minutes or until tender. Stir once or twice during cooking. Add the mushrooms and cook for 10 minutes.

4 Mix together the self-raising flour, pinch of salt and the suet. Mix together with 150–200 ml (5–7 fl oz) water to make a dough. Roll out two-thirds of the pastry and use to line a 1.2 litre (2 pint) greased basin. Make a lid with the remainder.

5 Spoon the meat and gravy into the basin. Damp the pastry edges and seal on the pastry lid. Cover loosely with cling film. Cook on High for 9 minutes. Remove the cling film. Wrap a napkin around the bowl and serve at once with creamed potatoes and spring greens, if wished.

STUFFED LOIN OF LAMB

SERVES ▶	4–6
SETTING ▶	HIGH
TIME ▶	19 MINUTES
GRADING ▶	LESS EASY

1 medium onion, skinned and chopped

50–75 g (2–3 oz) fresh white breadcrumbs

5 ml (1 level tsp) concentrated mint sauce

50 g (2 oz) raisins

25 g (1 oz) desiccated coconut

salt and pepper

1 egg, size 2, lightly beaten

900 g (2 lb) boned loin of lamb

25 g (1 oz) butter or margarine

watercress or fresh mint, to garnish

1 Put the onion in a 1.2 litre (2 pint) bowl, cover with cling film, pulling back one corner to allow steam to escape and cook for 3 minutes until tender.

2 Mix together the breadcrumbs, mint, raisins, coconut, salt and pepper. Bind the mixture with the egg.

3 Lay the loin, skin downwards, on a flat surface. Spread on the butter. Cover evenly with the stuffing.

4 Roll up the loin and secure tightly with string. Stand on a trivet in a shallow dish. Cook, uncovered, for 16 minutes. Turn the joint around halfway through cooking.

5 Retain the juices for the gravy. Wrap the joint tightly in foil and allow it to stand for 15 minutes. If a crisper skin is preferred, place the joint in a conventional oven, preheated to 190°C (375°F) mark 5 and cook for 15–20 minutes.

6 Remove the string and place the loin on a warmed serving dish. Garnish with watercress or fresh mint. Serve hot with roast potatoes and vegetables or cold with salad, if you wish.

CURRIED LEFTOVER MEAT

SERVES ▶	4
SETTING ▶	HIGH
TIME ▶	20 MINUTES
GRADING ▶	LESS EASY

1 medium onion, skinned and chopped

1 cooking apple, peeled, cored and chopped

15 ml (1 level tbsp) curry powder

1.25 ml ($\frac{1}{4}$ level tsp) chilli powder

1.25 ml ($\frac{1}{4}$ level tsp) ground cumin

25 g (1 oz) butter or margarine

15 ml (1 level tbsp) plain flour

15 ml (1 level tbsp) tomato purée

15 ml (1 tbsp) lemon juice

2.5 ml ($\frac{1}{2}$ level tsp) meat extract

227 g (8 oz) can chopped tomatoes with juice

300 ml ($\frac{1}{2}$ pint) hot beef, lamb or chicken stock

salt and pepper

700 g (1$\frac{1}{2}$ lb) cooked boneless meat, chopped

boiled rice, to serve (see page 86)

sliced tomatoes and lemon slices, to garnish

1 Put the onion, apple, curry powder, chilli powder, ground cumin and butter in a 2.75 litre (4$\frac{1}{2}$–5 pint) bowl. Cover with cling film, pulling back one corner to allow steam to escape and cook for 5 minutes. Stir halfway through cooking.

2 Stir in the flour. Blend in the tomato purée, lemon juice, meat extract, tomatoes and juice, hot stock, salt, pepper and chopped meat. Cook, covered with cling film as before, for 15 minutes until hot. Stir several times during cooking.

3 Serve on a warmed serving dish with boiled rice. Garnish with sliced tomatoes and lemon slices. Serve with desiccated coconut, chutney, sliced bananas and poppadums, if wished.

——— TIP ———

USE THE MICROWAVE TO COOK POPPADUMS. COOK 4 AT A TIME. PLACE ON A PIECE OF PAPER ON THE FLOOR OF THE COOKING CAVITY. COOK FOR 1$\frac{1}{2}$ MINUTES, THEN STAND FOR 1 MINUTE UNTIL CRISP. CHECK FREQUENTLY TO AVOID OVERCOOKING.

LAMB NOISETTES WITH VEGETABLES

SERVES ▶ 4	
SETTING ▶ HIGH and DEFROST	
TIME ▶ 33 MINUTES	
GRADING ▶ LESS EASY	

225 g (8 oz) potatoes, peeled and diced

100 g (4 oz) carrots, peeled and sliced

1 small onion, skinned and chopped

1 garlic clove, skinned and crushed

15 ml (1 tbsp) chopped fresh parsley

7.5 ml (1½ tsp) chopped fresh thyme

15 ml (1 level tbsp) tomato purée

15 g (½ oz) butter or margarine

8 lamb noisettes, 100 g (4 oz) each

150 ml (¼ pint) hot lamb stock

salt and pepper

1 Put the potatoes, carrots, onion, garlic, parsley, thyme, purée and butter in a 2.75 litre (4½–5 pint) bowl. Cover with cling film, pulling back one corner to allow steam to escape and cook for 8 minutes or until tender, stirring occasionally. Add the noisettes, hot stock, salt and pepper. Re-cover and cook for 10 minutes. Re-position halfway through cooking.

2 Reduce to Defrost. Cook, covered with cling film as before, for 15 minutes or until tender. Re-arrange halfway through cooking.

3 Remove the string from the noisettes and place on a warmed serving dish. Strain the vegetables, reserving the juice. Spoon the vegetables and a little of the strained sauce over each noisette.

MARINATED RUMP STEAKS

SERVES ▶ 4–6	
SETTING ▶ HIGH	
TIME ▶ 16 MINUTES	
GRADING ▶ LESS EASY	

4 rump steaks, 225 g (8 oz) each, lightly beaten

30 ml (2 tbsp) wine vinegar

150 ml (¼ pint) red wine

10 ml (2 level tsp) soft brown sugar

2 garlic cloves, skinned and crushed

1 medium onion, skinned and finely chopped

50 g (2 oz) butter or margarine

15 ml (1 tbsp) chopped fresh tarragon

salt and pepper

5 ml (1 level tsp) cornflour

fresh tarragon, to garnish

1 Place the steaks in a shallow dish. Mix together the vinegar, red wine, sugar, garlic and onion. Spread over the steaks. Cover and refrigerate for at least 7 hours. Turn several times during the marinating process.

2 Remove the steaks and cut into strips. Put the marinade with the onion in a large bowl, add the butter, tarragon, salt and pepper. Cover with cling film, pulling back one corner to allow steam to escape and cook for 5 minutes or until the onion is tender.

3 Stir in the steak. Re-cover and cook for 8 minutes. Stir halfway through cooking. If the meat is required medium rare, reduce cooking time by 2 minutes.

4 Place the steak in a warmed serving dish. Keep warm.

5 Mix together the cornflour and 30 ml (2 tbsp) water to make a smooth paste. Stir the paste into the remaining sauce. Cook, uncovered, for 3 minutes or until the sauce is thick. Stir every minute. Pour the sauce over the steaks. Garnish with fresh tarragon. Serve with new potatoes and a mixed salad, if wished.

SWEETBREADS IN WHITE WINE SAUCE

SERVES ▶ 4	
SETTING ▶ HIGH and using a conventional hob	
TIME ▶ 27½ MINUTES	
GRADING ▶ LESS EASY	

900 g (2 lb) sweetbreads

5 ml (1 tsp) malt vinegar

1.1 litres (2 pints) boiling water

2 rashers streaky bacon, rinded and chopped

½ red pepper, cored, seeded and diced

100 g (4 oz) mushrooms, chopped

1 celery stick, chopped

50 g (2 oz) butter or margarine, cut into pieces

1 bay leaf

25 ml (1½ level tbsp) plain flour

150 ml (¼ pint) dry white wine

150 ml (¼ pint) hot chicken stock

5 ml (1 level tsp) mustard powder

salt and pepper

15 ml (1 tbsp) lemon juice

30 ml (2 tbsp) double cream

boiled rice, to serve (see page 86)

chopped fresh parsley, to garnish

1 Soak the sweetbreads for 2 hours in lukewarm water, to which the vinegar has been added. Change the water once during soaking. Remove the fat and skin. Put the sweetbreads in a medium bowl. Pour in the boiling water. Cook, uncovered, for 8 minutes. Drain and plunge the sweetbreads into cold water. Stand for 10 minutes. Drain and set aside until cold.

2 Put the bacon, pepper, mushrooms, celery, butter and bay leaf in a 2.75 litre (4½–5 pint) bowl. Cover with cling film, pulling back one corner to allow steam to escape and cook for 6 minutes.

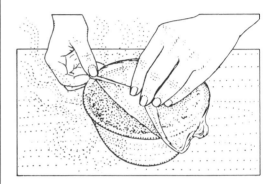

Stir in the flour and cook, uncovered, for 30 seconds. Gradually blend in the wine, hot stock, mustard, salt and pepper. Cook, uncovered, for 4 minutes. Stir every minute. Liquidise in a blender of food processor until smooth.

3 Pour the sauce back into the bowl. Add the sweetbreads. Re-cover and cook for 9 minutes or until hot. Stir halfway through cooking. Stir in the lemon juice and cream.

4 Arrange a bed of rice on a warmed serving dish. Spoon the sweetbread mixture into the centre. Garnish with chopped parsley and serve with carrots, if wished.

——— TIP ———

THE PREPARATION OF THE SWEETBREADS IN STEP 1 CAN BE USED FOR MOST SWEETBREAD RECIPES.

VEGETABLES

MICROWAVE COURSE GUIDANCE NOTES

Very small amounts of water should be used when cooking fresh raw vegetables:

45–60 ml (3–4 tbsp) for 450 g (1 lb) vegetables.

Like all foods cooked by microwave energy, vegetables should not be overcooked.

Unless instructions are given to the contrary, always cover the container with cling film, pulling back one corner to allow steam to escape.

Most vegetables tend to have a crisp texture when cooked. If very soft vegetables are required, use the conventional method of cooking.

If possible arrange vegetables with the delicate parts so that they are in the centre of the container, for example broccoli florets, asparagus tips.

Before cooking, prick or score any vegetable which has a skin to prevent it bursting, such as tomatoes, potatoes.

Always stir vegetables or rearrange halfway through cooking.

Never deep-fry vegetables in the microwave cooker.

Do not add any extra water when cooking frozen vegetables unless specifically instructed by the manufacturer.

If baking whole vegetable, such as potatoes in their jackets (see page 73), arrange them in a circle with a space between each. Avoid putting one in the centre.

HEATING CANNED VEGETABLES

SERVES ▶	2
SETTING ▶	HIGH
TIME ▶	3½ MINUTES
GRADING ▶	VERY EASY

300 g (10.6 oz) can vegetables, drained

Put the vegetables in a 1 litre (1¾ pint) bowl. Cover with cling film, pulling back one corner to allow steam to escape and cook for 3½ minutes or until hot.

——————— TIP ———————

THIS TIMING IS SUITABLE FOR CANNED VEGETABLES SUCH AS PEAS, BEANS, SLICED CARROTS AND MIXED VEGETABLES. IF HEATING WHOLE POTATOES 1–2 EXTRA MINUTES WILL BE NEEDED.

BROCCOLI WITH LEMON

SERVES ▶	4
SETTING ▶	HIGH
TIME ▶	12–13 MINUTES
GRADING ▶	EASY

700 g (1½ lb) broccoli, florets

25 g (1 oz) butter or margarine

1 small onion, skinned and finely chopped

1 garlic clove, skinned and crushed (optional)

grated rind and juice of 1 lemon

150 ml (¼ pint) chicken stock

salt and pepper

1 Put the butter, onion and garlic into a 2.75 litre (4½–5 pint) bowl. Cover with cling film, pulling back one corner to let steam escape and cook for 5 minutes until the onions are tender.

2 Place the broccoli on top of the onion and sprinkle it with the lemon rind and juice. Pour in the stock.
   Recover and cook for 7–8 minutes until the broccoli is tender. Stir halfway through cooking. Season with salt and pepper.

BUTTERED FROZEN PEAS

SERVES ▶	4
SETTING ▶	HIGH
TIME ▶	7–9 MINUTES
GRADING ▶	EASY

450 g (1 lb) frozen peas

25 g (1 oz) butter or margarine, cut into pieces

salt and pepper

1 Put the peas in a 2 litre (3½ pint) bowl. Cover with cling film, pulling back one corner to allow steam to escape and cook for 7–9 minutes. Stir halfway through cooking. Stand, covered, for 4 minutes.

2 Drain the peas. Toss in the butter until melted. Season with salt and pepper.

——————— TIPS ———————

FOR MINTED PEAS, ADD 5 ml (1 tsp) CHOPPED FRESH MINT TO THE PEAS BEFORE COOKING.

FOR MUSHY PEAS, DO NOT DRAIN. LIQUIDISE IN A BLENDER OR FOOD PROCESSOR WITH THE BUTTER, SALT AND PEPPER.

BOILED POTATOES

SERVES ▶ 4
SETTING ▶ HIGH
TIME ▶ 9–14 MINUTES
GRADING ▶ EASY

700 g (1½ lb) medium old potatoes, peeled and cut in half or new potatoes, scrubbed

salt and pepper

25 g (1 oz) butter or margarine, cut into pieces

chopped fresh parsley, to garnish

1 Put the potatoes and 45 ml (3 tbsp) water in a 2.75 litre (4½–5 pint) bowl. Cover with cling film, pulling back one corner to allow steam to escape and cook old potatoes for 10–14 minutes or new potatoes for 9–12 minutes or until tender. Stir halfway through cooking.

2 Drain the potatoes. Season with salt and pepper and toss in the butter. Spoon into a warmed serving dish. Garnish with chopped parsley.

————— TIPS —————

FOR MASHED POTATOES, DRAIN AND MASH WITH THE BUTTER, 60–75 ml (4–5 tbsp) MILK, SALT AND PEPPER.

FOR POTATO SALAD, CUT THE PEELED POTATOES INTO 2.5 CM (1 INCH) CUBES BEFORE COOKING. ALLOW TO COOL, THEN DRAIN AND TOSS IN MAYONNAISE.

FOR ROAST POTATOES, DRAIN THE POTATOES AFTER COOKING AND FRY IN SHALLOW OR DEEP FAT ON THE CONVENTIONAL HOB, TURNING FREQUENTLY UNTIL CRISP AND BROWN.

JACKET POTATOES

SERVES ▶ 4
SETTING ▶ HIGH
TIME ▶ 16 MINUTES
GRADING ▶ VERY EASY

4 medium potatoes, washed, dried and pricked

30 ml (2 tbsp) milk or single cream

salt and pepper

25 g (1 oz) butter or margarine

parsley sprigs, to garnish

1 Arrange the potatoes in a circle on a piece of absorbent kitchen paper. Cook, uncovered, for 13 minutes. Turn over halfway through cooking.

2 Wrap each potato tightly in kitchen foil and stand for 5 minutes.

3 Cut each potato lengthways. Scoop out the flesh. Mix the flesh with the milk or cream, salt, pepper and butter.

4 Pile the mixture back into the potato jackets. Cook, uncovered, for 3 minutes or until hot. Garnish with sprigs of parsley.

GLAZED CARROTS

SERVES ▶ 4	
SETTING ▶ HIGH	
TIME ▶ 9 MINUTES	
GRADING ▶ EASY	

50 g (2 oz) butter or margarine, cut into pieces

10 ml (2 level tsp) soft dark brown sugar

450 g (1 lb) young carrots, peeled and thinly sliced

salt and pepper

15 ml (1 tbsp) chopped fresh parsley, to garnish

1 Put the butter and sugar in a 2 litre (3½ pint) bowl. Cook, uncovered, for 1 minute.

2 Stir in the carrots. Cover with cling film, pulling back one corner to allow steam to escape and cook for 8 minutes. Leave to stand, covered, for 3 minutes. Season with salt and pepper.

3 Serve in a warmed serving dish. Garnish with chopped parsley.

——— TIP ———

OLD CARROTS CAN TOUGHEN WHILE COOKING, SO IT IS BETTER TO USE YOUNG CARROTS.

MANGE-TOUT WITH BUTTER

SERVES ▶ 4	
SETTING ▶ HIGH	
TIME ▶ 8 MINUTES	
GRADING ▶ EASY	

350 g (¾ lb) mange-tout, trimmed and strings removed

salt and pepper

25 g (1 oz) butter or margarine, cut into pieces

1 Put the mange-tout and 45 ml (3 tbsp) water in a 2.75 litre (4½–5 pint) bowl. Cover with cling film, pulling back one corner to allow steam to escape and cook for 8 minutes. Stir halfway through cooking.

2 Stand, covered, for 5 minutes. Drain the mange-tout. Season with salt and pepper, then toss the mange-tout in the butter until melted. Spoon into a warmed serving dish and garnish with a knob of butter, if wished.

STUFFED MARROW

SERVES ▶ 4
SETTING ▶ HIGH and using a conventional grill
TIME ▶ $31\frac{3}{4}$ MINUTES
GRADING ▶ LESS EASY

700 g ($1\frac{1}{2}$ lb) marrow, halved lengthways and
   seeds removed

2 garlic cloves, skinned and crushed

1 medium onion, skinned and finely chopped

2 tomatoes, skinned and chopped

2 mushrooms, finely chopped

2.5 ml ($\frac{1}{2}$ tsp) chopped fresh parsley or 1.25 ml
   ($\frac{1}{4}$ level tsp) dried

2.5 ml ($\frac{1}{2}$ tsp) chopped fresh rosemary or
   1.25 ml ($\frac{1}{4}$ level tsp) dried

75 g (3 oz) fresh brown breadcrumbs

225 g (8 oz) cooked ham, finely chopped

15 ml (1 level tbsp) tomato purée

5 ml (1 tsp) dry sherry

salt and pepper

25 g (1 oz) butter or margarine

25 g (1 oz) plain flour

300 ml ($\frac{1}{2}$ pint) milk

40 g ($1\frac{1}{2}$ oz) Cheddar cheese, finely grated

1 Put the marrow in a shallow dish. Cover with
   cling film, pulling back one corner to allow steam
to escape and cook for 14 minutes. Drain and cover.

2 Put the garlic, onion, tomatoes, mushrooms,
   parsley and rosemary in a 2.75 litre ($4\frac{1}{2}$–5 pint)
bowl. Cover with cling film, pulling back one corner
to allow steam to escape and cook for 5 minutes.
Stir in the breadcrumbs, ham, tomato purée, sherry,
salt and pepper. Re-cover and cook for 4 minutes.
Set aside, covered.

3 Put the butter in a 600 ml (1 pint) jug. Cook,
   uncovered, for 45 seconds or until melted.
Blend in the flour and cook, uncovered, for 30
seconds. Gradually blend in the milk, add salt and
pepper. Cook, uncovered, for 4 minutes or until
thickened. Stir every minute.

4 Fill the marrow halves with the stuffing, spoon
   the sauce over it and reheat for $3\frac{1}{2}$ minutes.
Sprinkle the cheese over the sauce and brown
under a preheated grill.

FENNEL WITH WHITE SAUCE

SERVES ▶ 4
SETTING ▶ HIGH
TIME ▶ $13\frac{1}{4}$ MINUTES
GRADING ▶ LESS EASY

450 g (1 lb) fennel bulbs, top stems trimmed
   and base removed, thinly sliced

25 g (1 oz) butter or margarine

25 g (1 oz) plain flour

300 ml ($\frac{1}{2}$ pint) milk

salt and pepper

sprigs of fennel, to garnish

1 Put the fennel and 60 ml (4 tbsp) water in a
   2 litre ($3\frac{1}{2}$ pint) bowl. Cover with cling film,
pulling back one corner to allow steam to escape and
cook for 8 minutes. Stir halfway through cooking. Set
aside, covered, while making the sauce.

2 Put the butter in a 600 ml (1 pint) jug. Cook,
   uncovered, for 45 seconds or until melted. Stir
in the flour and cook, uncovered, for 30 seconds.
Gradually blend in the milk. Cook, uncovered, for 4
minutes or until thickened. Stir every minute. Season
with salt and pepper.

3 Drain the fennel and put into a warmed serving
   dish. Reheat if necessary. Pour the sauce over
the fennel. Garnish with sprigs of fennel leaves.

CAULIFLOWER POLONAISE

SERVES ▶ 4	
SETTING ▶ HIGH and using a conventional hob	
TIME ▶ 10 MINUTES	
GRADING ▶ LESS EASY	

1 cauliflower, prepared weight 700 g (1½ lb)

50 g (2 oz) butter or margarine

50 g (2 oz) dried white breadcrumbs

15 ml (1 tbsp) chopped fresh parsley

salt and pepper

15 ml (1 tbsp) lemon juice

*2 hard-boiled eggs, yolks and whites sieved
separately, to garnish*

1 Rinse the cauliflower in water, and make an incision in the base of the stalk. Put in a 2 litre (3½ pint) bowl. Cover with cling film, pulling back one corner to allow steam to escape and cook for 10 minutes until tender. Turn over halfway through cooking.

2 Meanwhile, put the butter in a conventional frying pan. Using the conventional hob, melt the butter and fry the breadcrumbs until golden brown. Stir in the parsley, salt, pepper and lemon juice.

3 Drain the cauliflower. Arrange in a warmed serving dish. Sprinkle with the breadcrumbs. Garnish with a pattern of sieved egg yolk and sieved egg white.

JERUSALEM ARTICHOKES

SERVES ▶ 4	
SETTING ▶ HIGH	
TIME ▶ 9 MINUTES	
GRADING ▶ EASY	

*450 g (1 lb) Jerusalem artichokes, scrubbed or
peeled and sliced*

salt and pepper

25 g (1 oz) butter or margarine, cut into pieces

chopped parsley, to garnish

1 Put the artichokes and 45 ml (3 tbsp) water in a 2 litre (3½ pint) bowl. Cover with cling film, pulling back one corner to allow steam to escape and cook for 9 minutes until tender. Stir halfway through cooking. Drain the artichokes.

2 Season with salt and pepper then toss in the butter. Spoon into a warmed serving dish. Sprinkle with parsley.

——— TIPS ———

FOR MASHED ARTICHOKES, LIQUIDISE IN A BLENDER OR FOOD PROCESSOR WITH THE BUTTER, SALT AND PEPPER AND 30–45 ml (2–3 tbsp) MILK.

LEEKS WITH WHITE SAUCE

SERVES ▶	4
SETTING ▶	HIGH
TIME ▶	$15\frac{1}{4}$ MINUTES
GRADING ▶	LESS EASY

550 g (1¼ lb) leeks, trimmed and finely sliced

25 g (1 oz) butter or margarine

25 g (1 oz) plain flour

300 ml (½ pint) milk

salt and pepper

chopped fresh parsley, to garnish

1 Put the leeks and 45 ml (3 tbsp) water in a 2.75 litre (4½–5 pint) bowl. Cover with cling film, pulling back one corner to allow steam to escape and cook for 10 minutes. Set aside, covered.

2 Put the butter in a 600 ml (1 pint) jug. Cook, uncovered, for 45 seconds or until melted. Stir in the flour and cook, uncovered, for 30 seconds. Gradually blend in the milk. Cook, uncovered, for 4 minutes, until boiled and thickened. Stir every minute. Season with salt and pepper.

3 Drain the leeks. Spoon into a warmed serving dish. Pour the sauce over the leeks and garnish with chopped parsley.

MINTED BRUSSELS SPROUTS

SERVES ▶	4
SETTING ▶	HIGH
TIME ▶	12 MINUTES
GRADING ▶	EASY

700 g (1½ lb) Brussels sprouts, trimmed with a cross slit into the base of each

5 ml (1 tsp) chopped fresh mint

salt and pepper

25 g (1 oz) butter or margarine, cut into pieces

1 Put the sprouts, mint and 45 ml (3 tbsp) water in a 2.75 litre (4½–5 pint) bowl. Cover with cling film and pull back one edge to allow steam to escape and cook for 12 minutes. Stir halfway through cooking.

2 Leave to stand, covered, for 5 minutes. Drain the sprouts. Season with salt and pepper, then toss the sprouts in the butter. Spoon into a warmed serving dish.

RED SPLIT LENTILS

SERVES ▶	4
SETTING ▶	HIGH
TIME ▶	20 MINUTES
GRADING ▶	EASY

1 medium onion, skinned and finely chopped

175 g (6 oz) red split lentils

600 ml (1 pint) hot vegetable stock

salt and pepper

25 g (1 oz) butter or margarine

1 Put the onion in a 2.75 litre (4½–5 pint) bowl. Cover with cling film, pulling back one corner to allow steam to escape and cook for 5 minutes.

2 Stir in the lentils and the hot stock. Re-cover and cook for 15 minutes. Do not remove the cling film during cooking.

3 Stand, covered, for 5 minutes. Season with salt and pepper, then stir in the butter until melted. Spoon into a warmed serving dish.

DICED SWEDE WITH PARSLEY

SERVES ▶	4
SETTING ▶	HIGH
TIME ▶	9 MINUTES
GRADING ▶	EASY

700 g (1½ lb) swede, peeled and cut into 1 cm (½ inch) cubes

salt and pepper

25 g (1 oz) butter or margarine, cut into pieces

15 ml (1 tbsp) chopped fresh parsley

1 Put the swede and 45 ml (3 tbsp) water in a 2.75 litre (4½–5 pint) bowl. Cover with cling film, pulling back one corner to allow steam to escape and cook for 9 minutes, until tender. Stir halfway through cooking. Drain.

2 Season with salt and pepper, then gently toss the swede in the butter and parsley. Spoon into a hot serving dish.

FROZEN SPINACH WITH NUTMEG

SERVES ▶	2
SETTING ▶	HIGH
TIME ▶	3¾ MINUTES
GRADING ▶	EASY

25 g (1 oz) butter or margarine

454 g (1 lb) packet frozen spinach

grated nutmeg

salt and pepper

1 Put the butter in a 2 litre (3½ pint) bowl and cook uncovered for 45 seconds or until melted. Add the spinach and cook, uncovered, for 3 minutes, or until hot. Stir halfway through cooking. Season with nutmeg, salt and pepper.

BEETROOT WITH
CAPERS

SERVES ▶ 4	
SETTING ▶ HIGH	
TIME ▶ $10\frac{3}{4}$ MINUTES	
GRADING ▶ EASY	

450 g (1 lb) raw beetroot

150 ml ($\frac{1}{4}$ pint) boiling water

25 g (1 oz) butter or margarine

5 ml (1 level tsp) granulated sugar

15 ml (1 level tbsp) capers

salt and pepper

1 Put the raw beetroot and water in a shallow dish. Cover with cling film, pulling back one corner to allow steam to escape and cook for 10 minutes or until tender, repositioning halfway through cooking. Set aside, covered.

2 Put the butter, sugar and capers in a 600 ml (1 pint) jug. Cook, uncovered, for 45 seconds or until the butter has melted.

3 Skin the beetroot and dice. Toss in the butter. Season with salt and pepper. Spoon into a warmed serving dish.

——— TIP ———
SERVE WITH HOT OR COLD MEATS.

COURGETTES WITH
TOMATOES

SERVES ▶ 4	
SETTING ▶ HIGH	
TIME ▶ 8 MINUTES	
GRADING ▶ EASY	

450 g (1 lb) courgettes, trimmed and sliced

1 garlic clove, skinned and crushed

100 g (4 oz) tomatoes, skinned and chopped

25 g (1 oz) butter or margarine

5 ml (1 level tsp) dried mixed herbs

30 ml (2 level tbsp) tomato purée

salt and pepper

1 Put the courgettes, garlic, tomatoes, butter, herbs and purée in a 2.75 litre ($4\frac{1}{2}$–5 pint) bowl. Cover with cling film, pulling back one corner to allow steam to escape and cook for 8 minutes or until tender. Stir halfway through cooking.

2 Season with salt and pepper. Spoon into a warmed serving dish.

BUTTERED MIXED VEGETABLES

SERVES ▶ 4
SETTING ▶ HIGH
TIME ▶ 8½ MINUTES
GRADING ▶ EASY

½ red pepper, cored, seeded and sliced

100 g (4 oz) young carrots, peeled and finely sliced

175 g (6 oz) leeks, trimmed and finely sliced

25 g (1 oz) butter or margarine

salt and pepper

1 Put the red pepper, carrots and 45 ml (3 tbsp) water in a 2.75 litre (4½–5 pint) bowl. Cover with cling film, pulling back one corner to allow steam to escape and cook for 3½ minutes.

2 Stir in the leeks. Re-cover and cook for 5 minutes until tender. Stir halfway through cooking, then drain.

3 Stir in the butter until melted. Season with salt and pepper. Spoon into a warmed serving dish.

CARROT AND POTATO PURÉE

SERVES ▶ 4
SETTING ▶ HIGH
TIME ▶ 9 MINUTES
GRADING ▶ LESS EASY

225 g (8 oz) young carrots, peeled and finely sliced

350 g (12 oz) potatoes, peeled and diced

25 g (1 oz) butter or margarine

75 ml (5 tbsp) milk

salt and pepper

grated carrot, to garnish

1 Put the carrots, potatoes and 60 ml (4 tbsp) water in a 2.75 litre (4½–5 pint) bowl. Cover with cling film, pulling back one corner to allow steam to escape and cook for 9 minutes or until tender. Stir halfway through cooking.

2 Stir in the butter until melted. Add the milk, salt and pepper.

3 Liquidise in a blender or food processor until smooth.

4 Spoon into a warmed serving dish. Garnish with grated carrot.

Opposite
Beef and Orange Casserole (page 67), *Mange-tout with Butter* (page 74)

Overleaf
Buttered Mixed Vegetables (page 80), *Cauliflower Polonaise* (page 76), *Courgettes with Tomatoes* (page 79)

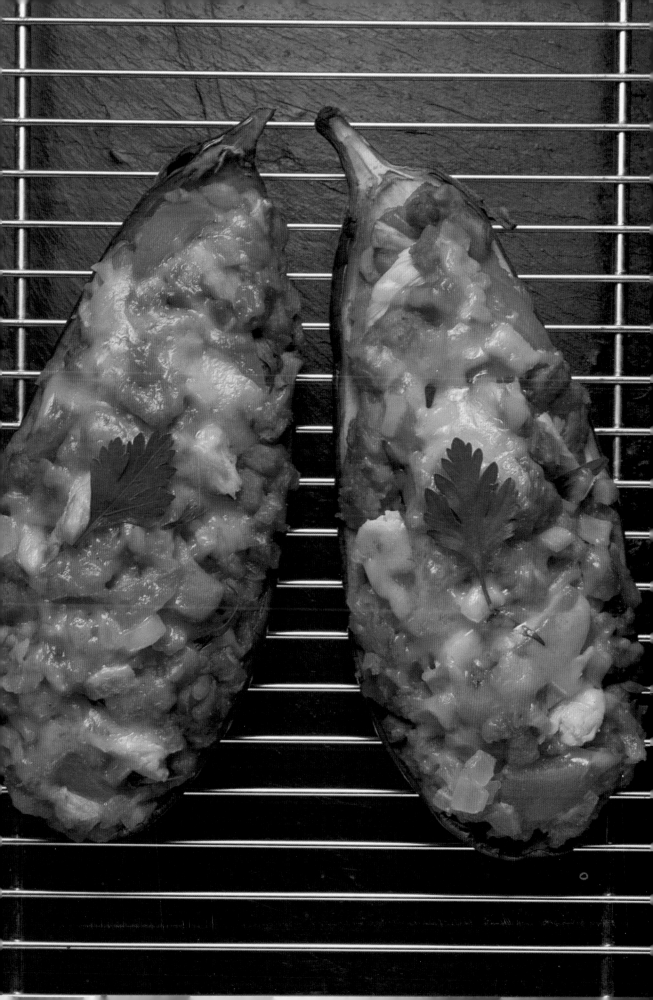

BRAISED LETTUCE

SERVES ▶ 4	
SETTING ▶ HIGH	
TIME ▶ 9 MINUTES	
GRADING ▶ EASY	

1 Iceberg lettuce, weighing about 700 g (1½ lb), stem removed and cut into 12 wedges

50 g (2 oz) butter or margarine, cut into small pieces

150 ml (¼ pint) hot chicken stock

salt and pepper

50 g (2 oz) Gruyère cheese, finely grated

paprika, to garnish

1 Put the lettuce, butter and stock in a 2.75 litre (4½–5 pint) bowl. Cover with cling film, pulling back one corner to allow steam to escape and cook for 7 minutes. Stir after 4 minutes.

2 Arrange the lettuce in a warmed ovenproof serving dish. Season with salt and pepper to taste and stir in the cheese.

3 Cook, uncovered, for 2 minutes or until the cheese has melted. Garnish with a sprinkle of paprika.

BUTTERED CABBAGE

SERVES ▶ 4	
SETTING ▶ HIGH	
TIME ▶ 8 MINUTES	
GRADING ▶ EASY	

350 g (12 oz) cabbage, stalk removed and finely shredded

40 g (1½ oz) butter or margarine, cut into pieces

pinch of grated nutmeg

salt and pepper

1 Put the cabbage and 45 ml (3 tbsp) water in a 2.75 litre (4½–5 pint) bowl. Cover with cling film, pulling back one corner to allow steam to escape and cook for 8 minutes until tender. Stir halfway through cooking.

2 Drain and stir in the butter until melted. Season with nutmeg and salt and pepper to taste.

Overleaf
Stuffed **A**ubergines (page 82)

Opposite
Paella (page 88)

STUFFED PEPPERS

SERVES ▶ 4
SETTING ▶ HIGH
TIME ▶ 24 MINUTES
GRADING ▶ LESS EASY

1 medium onion, skinned and very finely chopped

25 g (1 oz) butter or margarine, cut into pieces

2 garlic cloves, skinned and crushed

15 ml (1 level tbsp) tomato purée

2.5 ml ($\frac{1}{2}$ tsp) chopped fresh parsley or 1.25 ml ($\frac{1}{4}$ level tsp) dried

2.5 ml ($\frac{1}{2}$ tsp) chopped fresh basil or 1.25 ml ($\frac{1}{4}$ level tsp) dried

salt and pepper

100 g (4 oz) long grain rice

450 ml ($\frac{3}{4}$ pint) hot beef stock

50 g (2 oz) cooked boned chicken, minced

4 red peppers, cored, seeded and blanched

parsley sprigs, to garnish

1 Mix together the onion, butter, garlic, tomato purée, parsley, basil, salt and pepper in a 2.75 litre ($4\frac{1}{2}$–5 pint) bowl. Cover with cling film, pulling back one corner to allow steam to escape and cook for 5 minutes or until onions are tender.

2 Stir in the rice, hot stock and chicken. Re-cover and cook for 9 minutes. Set aside, covered, for 10 minutes.

3 Arrange the peppers in a shallow dish. Fill each pepper with some rice mixture. Cook, covered with cling film as before, for 10 minutes. Re-position halfway through cooking. Leave to stand, covered, for 5 minutes before serving. Garnish with parsley sprigs.

STUFFED AUBERGINES

SERVES ▶ 4
SETTING ▶ HIGH
TIME ▶ 15 MINUTES
GRADING ▶ LESS EASY

2 aubergines, each weighing about 800 g ($1\frac{3}{4}$ lb)

salt and pepper

1 medium onion, skinned and finely chopped

2 tomatoes, skinned and chopped

75 g (3 oz) butter or margarine, cut into pieces

30 ml (2 level tbsp) tomato purée

2 garlic cloves, skinned and crushed

15 ml (1 tbsp) chopped fresh tarragon or 5 ml (1 level tsp) dried

50 g (2 oz) fresh white breadcrumbs

50 g (2 oz) cooked ham, finely chopped

50 g (2 oz) cooked boned chicken, finely chopped

15 ml (1 tbsp) double cream or milk

50 g (2 oz) Cheddar cheese, finely grated

parsley sprigs, to garnish

1 Cut the aubergines in half lengthways. Sprinkle the cut edges with salt and set aside, inverted, to drain for 30 minutes. Rinse the aubergines in cold water and dry thoroughly on absorbent kitchen paper. Scoop out the flesh and dice. Reserve shells to serve.

2 Put the onion, tomatoes, butter, tomato purée, garlic, tarragon and diced aubergine in a 2.75 litre ($4\frac{1}{2}$–5 pint) bowl. Cover with cling film, pulling back one corner to allow steam to escape and cook for 6 minutes. Stir halfway through cooking.

3 Stir in the breadcrumbs, ham, chicken, salt and pepper. Add cream to bind. Divide the mixture between the reserved aubergine shells. Arrange in a shallow, ovenproof dish and cook, uncovered, for 6 minutes or until aubergines are tender. Reposition after 3 minutes.

4 Sprinkle the cheese over the top of the filled aubergines. Cook, uncovered, for 3 minutes or until the cheese has melted. Garnish with parsley.

SWEDE PURÉE

SERVES ▶	4
SETTING ▶	HIGH
TIME ▶	9 MINUTES
GRADING ▶	EASY

700 g (1½ lb) swede, peeled and cut into 1 cm (½ inch) cubes

25 g (1 oz) butter or margarine

15 ml (1 tbsp) double cream

salt and pepper

parsley sprig, to garnish

1 Put the swede and 45 ml (3 tbsp) water in a 2.75 litre (4½–5 pint) bowl. Cover with cling film, pulling back one corner to allow steam to escape and cook for 9 minutes. Stir halfway through cooking.

2 Put the swede, cooking liquid, butter, cream, salt and pepper in a blender or food processor and blend until smooth. Reheat, if necessary.

3 Place in a warmed serving dish. Garnish with a parsley sprig.

MIXED VEGETABLES WITH GARLIC

SERVES ▶	4
SETTING ▶	HIGH
TIME ▶	5 MINUTES
GRADING ▶	EASY

15 ml (1 tbsp) vegetable oil

1 garlic clove, skinned and crushed

1 green pepper, cored, seeded and sliced

3 courgettes, thinly sliced

100 g (4 oz) mushrooms, wiped and sliced

50 g (2 oz) frozen peas

5 spring onions, trimmed and finely sliced

15 ml (1 tbsp) soy sauce

salt and pepper

1 Put all the ingredients, except the soy sauce and seasoning, in a 2.75 litre (4½–5 pint) bowl. Cover with cling film, pulling back one corner to allow steam to escape and cook for 5 minutes, until the vegetables are just tender. Stir halfway through cooking.

2 Stir in the soy sauce and seasoning. Spoon into a warmed serving dish.

MICROWAVE COURSE GUIDANCE

Always use a large container to avoid the water boiling over.

When cooking rice or pasta always cover the container with cling film, pulling back one corner to allow steam to escape.

Cook brown rice the same way as white rice but allow a slightly longer cooking time.

Hot or boiling water should be used for cooking pasta and rice. It is quicker and more economical to use an electric kettle rather than the microwave cooker to heat the water.

During cooking ensure the rice and pasta is always covered by liquid.

After cooking allow a standing time as instructed with the cover still in position. Some pasta shapes take longer to cook than others.

15 ml (1 tbsp) vegetable oil added to the cooking water will help prevent the pasta sticking together.

Once pasta is tossed in a sauce it can be reheated quickly if necessary and will still retain its freshness.

COOKING

LASAGNE

SERVES ▶ 4	
SETTING ▶ HIGH	
TIME ▶ 9 MINUTES	
GRADING ▶ VERY EASY	

175 g (6 oz) lasagne

salt

15 ml (1 tbsp) vegetable oil

900 ml (1½ pints) boiling water

1 Put the lasagne, salt to taste and oil in a deep square or oblong casserole dish. Pour in the boiling water to cover the lasagne. Cover with cling film, pulling back one corner to allow steam to escape and cook for 9 minutes. Check periodically to ensure that the pasta is still covered with water.

2 Allow to stand, covered, for 10–15 minutes. Drain and use as required.

——— TIP ———

BEFORE USING THIS METHOD MAKE SURE THAT THE CONTAINER WILL ALLOW THE TURNTABLE TO ROTATE DURING COOKING.

COOKING

MACARONI

SERVES ▶ 4	
SETTING ▶ HIGH	
TIME ▶ 15 MINUTES	
GRADING ▶ VERY EASY	

225 g (8 oz) macaroni

15 ml (1 tbsp) vegetable oil

salt

1.1 litres (2 pints) boiling water

1 Put the macaroni, oil, salt to taste and boiling water in a 2.75 litre (4½–5 pint) bowl. Cover with cling film and cook for 15 minutes.

2 Allow to stand, covered, for 10 minutes. Drain and use as required.

COOKING

SPAGHETTI

SERVES ▶	4
SETTING ▶	HIGH
TIME ▶	9 MINUTES
GRADING ▶	VERY EASY

15 ml (1 tbsp) vegetable oil

salt

1.7 litres (3 pints) boiling water

225 g (8 oz) spaghetti

1 Put the oil, salt to taste and boiling water in a 2.75 litre ($4\frac{1}{2}$–5 pint) bowl. Stand the spaghetti in the bowl. Do not cover at this stage. Cook for 1 minute.

2 Gently push the softened spaghetti into the water so that the remaining hard strands are covered. Cover with cling film, pulling back one corner to allow steam to escape and cook for 8 minutes.

3 Allow to stand, covered, for 10 minutes. Drain and serve as usual.

——— TIP ———

THIS METHOD IS SUITABLE FOR ALL PASTAS EXCEPT LASAGNE, MACARONI (SEE RECIPES) AND CANNELLONI. CANNELLONI IS BEST COOKED AS A PART OF A DISH IN A SAUCE.

COOKING RICE

SERVES ▶	4
SETTING ▶	HIGH
TIME ▶	13 MINUTES
GRADING ▶	VERY EASY

225 g (8 oz) long grain rice

2.5 ml ($\frac{1}{2}$ tsp) vegetable oil

salt

750 ml ($1\frac{1}{4}$ pints) boiling water

1 Put the rice, oil, salt to taste and boiling water in a 2.75 litre ($4\frac{1}{2}$–5 pint) bowl. Cover with cling film, pulling back one corner to allow steam to escape and cook for 13 minutes. Stir halfway through cooking.

2 Allow to stand, covered, for 10 minutes before fluffing up with a fork.

——— TIPS ———

FOR A SAVOURY RICE USE BOILING MEAT, VEGETABLE OR FISH STOCK INSTEAD OF WATER, IF WISHED.

BROWN RICE OR UNTREATED RICE WILL REQUIRE A LONGER COOKING TIME AND MORE BOILING WATER. IN SUCH CASES THE CONVENTIONAL COOKING METHOD MAY BE PREFERRED.

BEEF LASAGNE

SERVES ▶ 4	
SETTING ▶ HIGH and using a conventional grill	
TIME ▶ 23½ MINUTES	
GRADING ▶ LESS EASY	

175 g (6 oz) lasagne

15 ml (1 tbsp) vegetable oil

salt and pepper

900 ml (1½ pints) boiling water

1 medium onion, skinned and finely chopped

2 garlic cloves, skinned and crushed

350 g (12 oz) minced beef

15 ml (1 level tbsp) tomato purée

2.5 ml (½ tsp) chopped fresh parsley

2.5 ml (½ tsp) chopped fresh thyme

100 g (4 oz) mushrooms, sliced

40 g (1½ oz) butter or margarine

40 g (1½ oz) plain flour

300 ml (½ pint) milk

150 ml (¼ pint) hot beef stock

50 g (2 oz) Parmesan cheese, finely grated

1 Put the lasagne, oil and salt to taste in a 5 cm (2 inch) deep oblong casserole dish. Pour over the boiling water, making sure the lasagne is completely submerged. Cover with cling film, pulling back one corner to allow steam to escape and cook for 9 minutes. Set aside, covered, for 15 minutes.

2 Meanwhile, put the onion, garlic, beef, purée, parsley, thyme, mushrooms, salt and pepper in a 2.75 litre (4½–5 pint) bowl. Cover with cling film and cook for 8 minutes. Stir halfway through cooking. Set aside, covered.

3 Put the butter in a 1 litre (1¾ pint) jug. Cook, uncovered, for 45 seconds or until melted. Blend in the flour and cook, uncovered, for 30 seconds. Gradually stir in the milk and stock. Cook, uncovered, for 4 minutes. Stir every minute.

4 Drain the lasagne. In an overproof dish, place half the lasagne over the base. Cover with the meat mixture. Pour over half the sauce. Cover with the remaining lasagne, then the remaining sauce. Sprinkle with the Parmesan cheese. Cook, uncovered, for 1¼ minutes, then brown under a preheated grill, if wished.

MACARONI CHEESE

SERVES ▶ 4	
SETTING ▶ HIGH and using a conventional grill	
TIME ▶ 22¼ MINUTES	
GRADING ▶ EASY	

225 g (8 oz) macaroni

15 ml (1 tbsp) vegetable oil

1.1 litres (2 pints) boiling water

salt and pepper

50 g (2 oz) butter or margarine

50 g (2 oz) plain flour

568 ml (1 pint) milk

2.5 ml (½ level tsp) prepared mustard

65 g (2½ oz) Parmesan cheese, finely grated

65 g (2½ oz) Cheddar cheese, finely grated

paprika, to garnish

1 Put the macaroni in a 2.75 litre (4½–5 pint) bowl. Add the oil and salt to taste and pour over the boiling water, making sure the macaroni is completely submerged in the water. Cover with cling film, pulling back one corner to allow steam to escape and cook for 15 minutes. Set aside, covered, for 10 minutes before draining.

2 Meanwhile, put the butter in a 1 litre (1¾ pint) jug. Cook, uncovered, for 45 seconds or until the butter is melted. Stir in the flour and cook, uncovered, for 30 seconds. Gradually blend in the milk, mustard, salt and pepper. Cook, uncovered, for 6 minutes or until thick. Stir after 2, 4 and 5 minutes.

3 Mix together the Parmesan and Cheddar cheeses. Stir 75 g (3 oz) of the cheeses into the sauce and fold into the drained macaroni. Pour the mixture into a flameproof dish. Sprinkle the remaining cheese over the top.

4 Brown under a preheated grill. Sprinkle with paprika to garnish.

PAELLA

SERVES ▶ 4
SETTING ▶ HIGH and using a conventional hob
TIME ▶ 31 MINUTES
GRADING ▶ LESS EASY

1 large onion, skinned and finely chopped

½ red pepper, cored, seeded and diced

2 garlic cloves, skinned and crushed

350 g (12 oz) long-grain rice

750 ml (1¼ pints) boiling chicken stock

salt

1.25 ml (¼ tsp) olive oil

few strands of saffron

4 chicken drumsticks

100 g (4 oz) frozen peas

175 g (6 oz) cooked prawns, peeled

175 g (6 oz) cooked mussels

100 g (4 oz) cooked boned pork, diced

2 tomatoes, skinned and chopped

cooked prawns in shells, to garnish

1 Put the onion, pepper and garlic in a 2.75 litre (4½–5 pint) bowl. Cover with cling film, pulling back one corner to allow steam to escape and cook for 6 minutes. Stir in the rice, stock, salt, oil and saffron. Re-cover and cook for 13 minutes. Stir halfway through cooking. Set aside, covered, for 10–14 minutes.

2 Meanwhile, brown the drumsticks in a frying pan on a conventional hob, then place in a 2 litre (3½ pint) bowl. Cover with cling film, pulling back one corner to allow steam to escape and cook for 5 minutes. Reposition halfway through cooking. Add the peas, prawns, mussels, pork and tomatoes. Re-cover and cook for 7 minutes or until hot. Remove the cooked chicken and keep warm.

3 Stir the cooked mixture into the rice. Pile on to a warmed serving dish. Arrange the chicken drumsticks on the top. Garnish with cooked prawns in their shells.

SPINACH STUFFED CANNELLONI

SERVES ▶ 4
SETTING ▶ HIGH
TIME ▶ 19 MINUTES
GRADING ▶ LESS EASY

450 g (1 lb) fresh spinach, washed, trimmed and drained

salt and pepper

12 cannelloni

900 g (2 lb) tomatoes

30 ml (2 level tbsp) tomato purée

60 ml (4 tbsp) olive oil

2 garlic cloves, skinned and crushed

50 g (2 oz) mushrooms

7.5 ml (½ tbsp) chopped fresh oregano or 5 ml (1 level tsp) dried

30 ml (2 tbsp) single cream

45–60 ml (3–4 level tbsp) finely grated Parmesan cheese

1 Put the spinach, with no extra water, in a 2.75 litre (4½–5 pint) bowl. Cover with cling film, pulling back one corner to let steam escape and cook for 6 minutes. Toss halfway through cooking. Drain, then chop in a blender or food processor. Turn into a sieve and squeeze out the excess water. Season to taste with salt and pepper.

2 Fill each cannelloni tube with the spinach. Arrange in the base of a shallow casserole dish. Choose one which will accommodate the cannelloni in one layer.

3 In a blender or food processor, blend the tomatoes, tomato purée, oil, garlic, mushrooms, salt, pepper, oregano and cream until smooth. Pour over the cannelloni, ensuring all the tubes are completely covered with the sauce. Cook, covered with cling film as before, for 9 minutes. Stir the sauce. Cook, uncovered, for 4 minutes or until cannelloni is tender. Stand, covered, for 5 minutes before serving. Sprinkle the cheese over the top.

——— TIP ———

SPRINKLE WITH THE CHEESE AND BROWN UNDER A PREHEATED GRILL, IF WISHED, BUT ENSURE THAT THE CASSEROLE DISH CAN WITHSTAND THE HEAT OF THE GRILL.

BROWN RICE
RISOTTO

SERVES ▶ 4
SETTING ▶ HIGH
TIME ▶ 38 MINUTES
GRADING ▶ LESS EASY

50 g (2 oz) butter or margarine

1 large onion, skinned and finely chopped

1 green pepper, cored, seeded and finely diced

15 ml (1 level tbsp) tomato purée

2 garlic cloves, skinned and crushed

salt and pepper

400 g (14 oz) brown long grain rice

900 ml (1½ pints) hot chicken stock

150 ml (¼ pint) dry white wine

100 g (4 oz) cooked boned chicken, chopped

50 g (2 oz) cooked ham, chopped

chopped fresh parsley, to garnish

1 Put the butter, onion, pepper, tomato purée, garlic, salt and pepper in a 2.75 litre (4½–5 pint) bowl. Cover with cling film, pulling back one corner to let steam escape and cook for 8 minutes. Stir halfway through cooking.

2 Stir in the rice, hot chicken stock, wine, chicken and ham. Re-cover and cook for 30 minutes. Leave to stand, covered, for 8–10 minutes before serving.

3 Pile on to a warmed serving dish. Garnish with chopped parsley.

SEMOLINA WEDGES

SERVES ▶ 4
SETTING ▶ HIGH, DEFROST
and using a conventional hob
TIME ▶ 11 MINUTES
GRADING ▶ LESS EASY

568 ml (1 pint) milk

150 g (5 oz) semolina

salt and pepper

5 ml (1 level tsp) mustard powder

2 egg yolks

plain flour, for coating

1 egg, beaten

dried breadcrumbs, for coating

vegetable oil, for deep fat frying

Tomato Sauce (see page 95), to serve

1 Put the milk in a 2 litre (3½ pint) bowl. Cook, uncovered, on High for 5 minutes or until boiling. Beat in the semolina. Reduce to Defrost. Cover with cling film, pulling back one corner to cook for 6 minutes. Beat and set aside to cool.

2 Beat the salt, pepper, mustard and the egg yolks into the cool semolina. Chill until firm. Divide into 12 pieces and with damp hands roll into cigar shapes. Toss each in flour, then egg and finally coat with the breadcrumbs. Lightly flatten each piece and shape into wedges.

3 Fry conventionally in preheated oil until golden brown. Drain on absorbent kitchen paper. Arrange the wedges on a warmed serving dish. Serve with freshly made Tomato Sauce, handed separately.

TAGLIATELLE WITH CREAM SAUCE

SERVES ▶	4
SETTING ▶	HIGH
TIME ▶	9 MINUTES
GRADING ▶	EASY

225 g (8 oz) tagliatelle

salt and pepper

15 ml (1 tbsp) vegetable oil

1.7 litres (3 pints) boiling water

2 eggs, lightly beaten

100 g (4 oz) butter or margarine, cut into small
pieces

60 ml (2½ fl oz) double cream

50 g (2 oz) Parmesan cheese, finely grated,
to garnish

1 Put the tagliatelle, salt to taste, oil and boiling
water in a 2.75 litre (4½–5 pint) bowl. Cover
with cling film and cook for 9 minutes. Check
occasionally to ensure the tagliatelle is completely
covered with the water during the cooking process.
Set aside, covered, for 8 minutes.

2 Drain the tagliatelle and toss it in the beaten
egg until the egg is set. (The heat of the
tagliatelle will cook the egg.) Toss in half the butter
and the cream and pepper.

3 Pile into a warm serving dish and dot with
the remaining butter. Garnish with the grated
Parmesan cheese.

CHEESE GNOCCHI

SERVES ▶	4
SETTING ▶ HIGH and using a conventional grill	
TIME ▶	13 MINUTES
GRADING ▶	EASY

10 ml (2 level tsp) cornflour

568 ml (1 pint) milk

100 g (4 oz) semolina

100 g (4 oz) Cheddar cheese, finely grated

salt and pepper

15 ml (1 level tbsp) brown breadcrumbs

25 g (1 oz) butter or margarine

parsley sprigs, to garnish

tomato sauce (see page 95), to serve

1 Blend the cornflour to a smooth paste with
30 ml (2 tbsp) of the milk. Put the remaining
milk in a 2.75 litre (4½–5 pint) bowl. Cook,
uncovered, for 5 minutes or until boiling. Whisk in
the semolina and cornflour mixture. Cover with cling
film, pulling back one corner to allow steam to
escape and cook for 5 minutes. Whisk after 3
minutes.

2 Beat in 75 g (3 oz) finely grated cheese until
melted. Season with salt and pepper. Spread in
a greased 18 × 20 cm (7 × 8 inch) tin. The mixture
should be about 2 cm (¾ inch) thick. Set aside until
cold.

3 Cut the gnocchi into 24 small squares. Overlap
the squares on a greased non-metallic flameproof
dish. Cook, uncovered, for 3 minutes.

4 Sprinkle the remaining cheese and breadcrumbs
over the top and dot with the butter. Place under
a preheated grill until brown. Serve immediately,
garnished with parsley. Hand the tomato sauce
separately.

NOODLES WITH NUTS

SERVES ▶	4
SETTING ▶	HIGH
TIME ▶	9 MINUTES
GRADING ▶	EASY

225 g (8 oz) tagliatelle

salt and pepper

15 ml (1 tbsp) vegetable oil

1.7 litres (3 pints) boiling water

350 g (12 oz) ricotta or curd cheese

2 garlic cloves, skinned and crushed

15 ml (1 tbsp) chopped fresh parsley

100 g (4 oz) walnuts, finely chopped

100 g (4 oz) Parmesan cheese, finely grated

25 g (1 oz) butter or margarine, cut into pieces

1 Put the tagliatelle, salt to taste, oil and boiling water in a 2.75 litre (4½–5 pint) bowl. Cover with cling film, pulling back one corner to allow steam to escape and cook for 9 minutes. Check during cooking that the noodles are completely immersed in water. Set aside, covered, for 8 minutes.

2 Meanwhile, mix together the ricotta cheese, garlic, parsley and walnuts. Stir in the Parmesan cheese and season with salt and pepper.

3 Drain the noodles. Toss the noodles in the butter, then the cheese and nut mixture. Serve on a warmed serving dish.

PASTA AND AVOCADO SALAD

SERVES ▶	4
SETTING ▶	HIGH
TIME ▶	9 MINUTES
GRADING ▶	EASY

175 g (6 oz) pasta spirals

1.1 litres (2 pints) boiling water

15 ml (1 tbsp) vegetable oil

salt and pepper

1.25 ml (¼ level tsp) mustard powder

45 ml (3 tbsp) olive oil

15 ml (1 tbsp) wine vinegar

2 celery sticks, finely chopped

½ green pepper, cored, seeded and diced

½ red pepper, cored, seeded and diced

2 garlic cloves, skinned and crushed

5 ml (1 tsp) chopped fresh parsley

15 ml (1 level tbsp) walnuts, chopped

2 avocados

1 Put the pasta, boiling water and oil in a 2.75 litre (4½–5 pint) bowl. Cover with cling film, pulling back one corner to allow steam to escape and cook for 9 minutes. Check during cooking that the pasta is completely immersed in the water. Leave to stand, covered, for 10 minutes. Drain. Rinse thoroughly with cold water. Drain thoroughly.

2 Put the salt, pepper and mustard in a small basin and mix them together with the oil. Whisk in the vinegar until well blended.

3 Skin the avocados, discard the stone and cut into small pieces. Mix together the celery, peppers, garlic, pepper, parsley, walnuts and vinaigrette dressing. Toss the pasta in the dressing and gently fold in the avocados. Serve in a bowl.

SAUCES

MICROWAVE COURSE GUIDANCE NOTES

Always use a container large enough to prevent the sauce boiling over. A jug is generally more convenient. For sauces up to 300 ml ($\frac{1}{2}$ pint) use a 600 ml (1 pint) jug; for sauces between 300 ml ($\frac{1}{2}$ pint) and 600 ml (1 pint) use a 1 litre ($1\frac{3}{4}$ pint) jug.

Unless instructions are given to the contrary, do not cover.

Stir sauces frequently to avoid lumps.

Egg and butter based sauces, such as Hollandaise, require very short microwave cooking and should be watched carefully to avoid curdling.

Sauces which require the addition of a raw egg or cheese can have these added after the cooking has been completed.

As microwave cooked sauces do not evaporate as much as conventionally cooked sauces, slightly less liquid can be used.

Large quantities of sauce, e.g. over 600 ml (1 pint), may be made more quickly and economically on a conventional hob.

BASIC WHITE SAUCE

SERVES ▶ 2–4 (makes 300 ml/½ pint)	
SETTING ▶ HIGH	
TIME ▶ $4\frac{1}{4}$–$5\frac{1}{4}$ MINUTES	
GRADING ▶ VERY EASY	

25 g (1 oz) butter or margarine

25 g (1 oz) plain flour

300 ml (½ pint) milk

salt and pepper

1 Put the butter in a 600 ml (1 pint) jug. Cook, uncovered, for 45 seconds or until the butter has melted.

2 Stir in the flour. Cook, uncovered, for 30 seconds. Gradually blend in the milk. Cook, uncovered for 3–4 minutes or until thick. Whisk every minute to avoid lumps forming. Season to taste with salt and pepper. Serve with vegetables, fish or poultry, if wished.

———— TIP ————

IF THE BUTTER AND MILK ARE AT ROOM TEMPERATURE THE COOKING TIME WILL BE SLIGHTLY FASTER.

———— VARIATIONS ————

PARSLEY SAUCE ADD 30 ml (2 tbsp) CHOPPED FRESH PARSLEY AND A DASH OF VINEGAR. SERVE WITH FISH.

ANCHOVY SAUCE ADD 5–10 ml (1–2 tsp) ANCHOVY ESSENCE AND A LITTLE RED COLOURING, IF WISHED. SERVE WITH FISH.

CHEESE SAUCE ADD 50 g (2 oz) GRATED HARD CHEESE AFTER THE WHITE SAUCE IS COOKED AND STIR UNTIL MELTED. SERVE WITH VEGETABLES, FISH OR MEAT.

MUSHROOM SAUCE ADD 25 g (1 oz) COOKED, CHOPPED MUSHROOMS. SERVE WITH MEAT, FISH OR VEGETABLES.

CURRY SAUCE ADD 5 ml (1 level tsp) CURRY POWDER. SERVE WITH MEAT, FISH OR VEGETABLES.

BASIC SWEET WHITE SAUCE

SERVES ▶ 2–4 (makes 300 ml/½ pint)	
SETTING ▶ HIGH	
TIME ▶ 3 MINUTES	
GRADING ▶ VERY EASY	

15 ml (1 level tbsp) cornflour

300 ml (½ pint) milk

15–30 ml (1–2 level tbsp) caster sugar

2 drops vanilla flavouring

knob of butter or margarine

1 Blend the cornflour with a little milk to make a smooth paste in a 600 ml (1 pint) jug. Stir in the remaining milk, sugar to taste and the vanilla flavouring.

2 Cook, uncovered, for 3 minutes or until thick. Whisk every minute. Stir in the butter until melted. Serve with puddings, fruit pies or stewed fruit, if wished.

———— VARIATIONS ————

ORANGE OR LEMON SAUCE STIR THE GRATED RIND OF 1 ORANGE OR 1 LEMON INTO THE MILK. SERVE WITH PUDDINGS, IF WISHED.

CHOCOLATE SAUCE STIR 15 ml (1 level tbsp) COCOA POWDER IN WITH THE CORNFLOUR. IF DRINKING CHOCOLATE POWDER IS USED LEAVE OUT THE SUGAR. SERVE WITH PUDDINGS.

COFFEE SAUCE SUBSTITUTE 150 ml (¼ pint) MILK WITH 150 ml (¼ pint) BLACK COFFEE. SERVE WITH PUDDINGS.

BÉCHAMEL SAUCE

SERVES ▶ 2–4 (makes 300 ml/½ pint)
SETTING ▶ HIGH
TIME ▶ 7¾ MINUTES
GRADING ▶ EASY

300 ml (½ pint) milk

1 small carrot, peeled and chopped

1 small celery stick, chopped

6 white peppercorns

blade of mace

1 bay leaf

25 g (1 oz) butter or margarine

25 g (1 oz) plain flour

30 ml (2 tbsp) double cream (optional)

salt

1 Put the milk, carrot, celery, peppercorns, mace and bay leaf in a 2 litre (3½ pint) bowl. Cook, uncovered, for 4 minutes. Cover and set aside to infuse for 10–15 minutes. Strain the milk, discarding the vegetables.

2 Put the butter in a 600 ml (1 pint) jug. Cook, uncovered, for 45 seconds or until melted. Stir in the flour and cook, uncovered, for 30 seconds. Gradually blend in the strained milk. Cook for 2½ minutes or until thick and smooth. Whisk every minute.

3 Stir in the cream, if used, and add salt to taste. Reheat if required but do not boil.

——— TIP ———
USE AS FOR BASIC WHITE SAUCE.

HOLLANDAISE SAUCE

SERVES ▶ 2–4 (makes about 75 ml/3 fl oz)
SETTING ▶ HIGH
TIME ▶ 1 MINUTE
GRADING ▶ LESS EASY

50 g (2 oz) butter or margarine

2 egg yolks, size 2

salt and pepper

15 ml (1 tbsp) lemon juice (optional)

1 Put 25 g (1 oz) of the butter in a 600 ml (1 pint) jug. Cook, uncovered, for 45 seconds or until melted. Beat in the egg yolks. Cook, uncovered, for 15 seconds. Beat hard until the sauce is smooth.

2 Cut the remaining butter into 8 pieces and beat into the mixture, one at a time. Add salt and pepper to taste. If a thinner consistency is required, beat in the lemon juice. Serve with asparagus, poached eggs or steaks, if wished.

TOMATO SAUCE

SERVES ▶	4–6 (makes 600 ml/1 pint)
SETTING ▶	HIGH
TIME ▶	10½ MINUTES
GRADING ▶	EASY

25 g (1 oz) butter or margarine

1 medium onion, skinned and finely chopped

½ rasher bacon, rinded and chopped

½ small carrot, peeled and grated

5 ml (1 level tsp) caster sugar

25 ml (1½ level tbsp) tomato purée

25 g (1 oz) plain flour

150 ml (¼ pint) hot chicken stock

550 g (1¼ lb) tomatoes, chopped

salt and pepper

1 Put the butter, onion, bacon, carrot, sugar and tomato purée in a 2.75 litre (4½–5 pint) bowl. Cover with cling film, pulling back one corner to allow steam to escape and cook for 5 minutes.

2 Stir in the flour and cook, uncovered, for 30 seconds. Gradually blend in the stock. Add the tomatoes, salt and pepper. Cover with cling film, pulling back one corner to allow steam to escape and cook for 5 minutes or until thick. Stir after 2, 3 and 4 minutes.

3 Liquidise in blender or food processor. Pass through a sieve. Reheat if necessary. Serve with meat, poultry or white fish, if wished.

BARBECUE SAUCE

SERVES ▶	2–4 (makes 300 ml/½ pint)
SETTING ▶	HIGH
TIME ▶	6 MINUTES
GRADING ▶	EASY

1 small onion, skinned and chopped

15 ml (1 level tbsp) cornflour

150 ml (¼ pint) hot vegetable stock

15 ml (1 level tbsp) tomato purée

15 ml (1 tbsp) white wine vinegar

10 ml (2 level tsp) mustard powder

15 ml (1 tbsp) Worcestershire sauce

15 ml (1 tbsp) soy sauce

30 ml (2 level tbsp) soft dark brown sugar

1 Put the onion in a 1 litre (1¾ pint) bowl. Cover with cling film, pulling back one corner to allow steam to escape and cook for 3 minutes.

2 Blend the cornflour with a little of the stock and stir into the onion with the remaining stock and the remaining ingredients. Cook, uncovered, for 3 minutes. Whisk every minute.

3 Liquidise in a blender or a food processor. Serve with meat, fish or poultry, if wished.

GRAVY

SERVES ▶	2–4 (makes 300 ml/½ pint)
SETTING ▶	HIGH
TIME ▶	4 MINUTES
GRADING ▶	VERY EASY

10 ml (2 level tsp) arrowroot or cornflour

300 ml (½ pint) poultry or meat stock

few drops of browning

salt and pepper

15 ml (1 tbsp) sherry (optional)

1 Put the arrowroot in a 600 ml (1 pint) jug and mix with a little of the stock until blended.

2 Mix together the remaining stock, browning, salt and pepper and sherry, if using. Cook, uncovered, for 3 minutes. Pour the liquid on to the arrowroot, stirring constantly. Cook, uncovered, for 1 minute or until the sauce is clear. Stir after 30 seconds. Strain and serve hot.

——— TIPS ———

USE THE COOKING JUICES FROM ROASTED MEAT OR POULTRY TO BE INCLUDED AS PART OF THE TOTAL STOCK QUANTITY.

BREAD SAUCE

SERVES ▶	2–4 (makes 350 ml/12 fl oz)
SETTING ▶	HIGH
TIME ▶	7 MINUTES
GRADING ▶	EASY

½ small onion, skinned and chopped

2 or 3 cloves

25 g (1 oz) butter or margarine

300 ml (½ pint) milk

50 g (2 oz) fresh white breadcrumbs

salt and pepper

1 Put the onion, cloves, butter and milk in a 1 litre (1¾ pint) jug. Cook, uncovered, for 4 minutes. Set aside for 10–15 minutes to infuse.

2 Strain the milk on to the breadcrumbs. Discard the onion and cloves. Cook, uncovered, for 3 minutes to heat. Stir every minute. Season with salt and pepper to taste. Serve with poultry, if wished.

ONION SAUCE

SERVES ▶	2–4 (makes 300 ml/½ pint)
SETTING ▶	HIGH
TIME ▶	10 MINUTES
GRADING ▶	VERY EASY

25 g (1 oz) butter or margarine

1 medium onion, skinned and finely chopped

25 g (1 oz) plain flour

300 ml (½ pint) milk

salt and pepper

1 Put the butter in a 2 litre (3½ pint) bowl and cook, uncovered, for 45 seconds or until melted. Stir in the onion and cook, uncovered, for 5 minutes or until the onion is tender.

2 Stir in the flour and cook, uncovered, for 30 seconds. Gradually blend in the milk and cook for 3 minutes, uncovered, whisking every minute. Season to taste with salt and pepper. Serve hot with roast meat, sausages, toad-in-the-hole and vegetable dishes.

Opposite
Beef **L**asagne (page 87)

Overleaf
Orange **S**orbet (page 112)

BASIC CUSTARD

SERVES ▶	2–4 (makes 300 ml ($\frac{1}{2}$ pint))
SETTING ▶	HIGH
TIME ▶	3 MINUTES
GRADING ▶	VERY EASY

15 ml (1 level tbsp) custard powder

15 ml (1 level tbsp) caster sugar

300 ml ($\frac{1}{2}$ pint) milk

1 Put the custard powder and sugar in a 600 ml (1 pint) jug. Stir in a little milk to make a smooth paste, then stir in the remaining milk.

2 Cook, uncovered, for 3 minutes or until thick. Stir every minute. Serve hot or cold with fruit pies, puddings, fruit and jellies, if wished.

GOOSEBERRY SAUCE

SERVES ▶	2 (makes 150 ml/$\frac{1}{4}$ pint)
SETTING ▶	HIGH
TIME ▶	6 MINUTES
GRADING ▶	EASY

450 g (1 lb) gooseberries, topped and tailed

25 g (1 oz) butter or margarine

45–60 ml (3–4 level tbsp) caster sugar

pinch of ground ginger (optional)

1 Put the gooseberries and 30 ml (2 tbsp) water in a 2 litre ($3\frac{1}{2}$ pint) bowl. Add the ginger, if used. Cover with cling film, pulling back one corner to let steam escape and cook for 6 minutes or until the fruit is soft. Add the butter or margarine and caster sugar and stir until the sugar has dissolved.

2 Rub the fruit with juice through a sieve to remove the seeds. Serve hot or cold with steamed puddings or ice cream.

Overleaf
***C**hocolate **C**ake* (page 114), ***F**lorentines* (page 115)

Opposite
***P**ickled **O**nions* (page 122), ***P**ickled **R**ed **C**abbage* (page 122), ***B**anana **C**hutney* (page 121)

EGG SAUCE

SERVES ▶	2–4 (makes 300 ml/$\frac{1}{2}$ pint)
SETTING ▶	HIGH
TIME ▶	4 MINUTES
GRADING ▶	LESS EASY

300 ml ($\frac{1}{2}$ pint) milk

few drops vanilla flavouring

25 g (1 oz) caster sugar

2 egg yolks, size 2

20–25 g ($\frac{3}{4}$–1 oz) cornflour (according to desired consistency)

1 Put the milk and vanilla flavouring in a 600 ml (1 pint) jug. Cook, uncovered, for 2 minutes.

2 Beat together the sugar, egg yolks and cornflour. Gradually beat the milk into the egg mixture.

3 Cook the sauce for 2 minutes or until thick and creamy. Whisk every 30 seconds. Serve with stewed fruit, puddings or fruit pies, if wished.

MARMALADE SAUCE

SERVES ▶ 2–4 (makes 300 ml/½ pint)	
SETTING ▶ HIGH	
TIME ▶ 4 MINUTES	
GRADING ▶ VERY EASY	

30 ml (2 level tbsp) orange marmalade

50 g (2 oz) caster sugar

5 ml (1 level tsp) arrowroot

juice of ½–1 orange

1 Stir the marmalade, sugar and 150 ml (¼ pint) water into a 1 litre (1¾ pint) bowl. Cook, uncovered, for 3 minutes.

2 Mix the arrowroot and 15 ml (1 tbsp) water to make a paste. Gradually add the marmalade liquid, stirring constantly. Cook, uncovered, for 1 minute until the sauce is clear. Stir halfway through cooking.

3 Adjust the consistency and flavour by adding orange juice. Do not strain. Serve with steamed puddings, if wished.

——— TIP ———
FOR DIFFERENTLY FLAVOURED SAUCES SUBSTITUTE JAMS
FOR THE MARMALADE.

APPLE SAUCE

SERVES ▶ 2–4 (makes 200 ml/7 fl oz)	
SETTING ▶ HIGH	
TIME ▶ 8 MINUTES	
GRADING ▶ EASY	

450 g (1 lb) cooking apples, peeled, cored and thinly sliced

small strip of lemon rind

3 cloves

15 ml (1 level tbsp) caster sugar

15 g (½ oz) butter or margarine

1 Put the apples, lemon rind, cloves, sugar, butter and 30 ml (2 tbsp) water in a 2.75 litre (4½–5 pint) bowl. Cover with cling film, pulling back one corner to allow steam to escape and cook for 5 minutes or until apples are tender. Stir halfway through cooking.

2 Remove the cloves and lemon rind and discard. In a blender or food processor liquidise the apple mixture until smooth. Return to the bowl.

3 Cook, uncovered, for 3 minutes if necessary to reheat. Serve with pork, if wished.

CHOCOLATE SAUCE

SERVES ▶ 2–4 (makes 200 ml/7 fl oz)
SETTING ▶ HIGH
TIME ▶ $2\frac{1}{4}$ MINUTES
GRADING ▶ EASY

50 g (2 oz) plain chocolate, grated

5 ml (1 level tsp) cornflour

100 ml (4 fl oz) milk

5 ml (1 level tsp) caster sugar

65 ml ($2\frac{1}{2}$ fl oz) double cream

2.5 ml ($\frac{1}{2}$ tsp) vanilla flavouring

1 Put the chocolate and 30 ml (2 tbsp) water in a 600 ml (1 pint) jug. Cook, uncovered, for 30 seconds or until melted.

2 Mix together the cornflour and milk to make a smooth paste. Stir into the chocolate mixture and add the sugar. Cook, uncovered, for $1\frac{3}{4}$ minutes or until thick. Stir every 30 seconds.

3 If serving the sauce hot, cool slightly before stirring in the cream and vanilla flavouring. Reheat if necessary, but do not boil.

4 If serving the sauce cold, cool before stirring in the cream and vanilla flavouring. Serve with steamed puddings, if wished.

——— TIP ———

IF PREFERRED, INCREASE THE QUANTITY OF MILK INSTEAD OF USING THE DOUBLE CREAM.

BUTTERSCOTCH SAUCE

SERVES ▶ 4 (makes 150 ml/$\frac{1}{4}$ pint)
SETTING ▶ HIGH
TIME ▶ 5 MINUTES
GRADING ▶ EASY

175 g (6 oz) can evaporated milk

75 g (3 oz) soft brown sugar

25 g (1 oz) butter or margarine

2.5 ml ($\frac{1}{2}$ tsp) vanilla flavouring

15 ml (1 level tbsp) cornflour

25 g (1 oz) raisins (optional)

1 Pour the evaporated milk into a 2 litre ($3\frac{1}{2}$ pint) bowl and add 30 ml (2 tbsp) water and the brown sugar. Cook, uncovered, for 3 minutes, stirring halfway through cooking. Add the butter or margarine and vanilla flavouring.

2 Blend the cornflour with a little cold water to make a smooth paste and add to the bowl. Cook for 2 minutes or until thick and smooth. Whisk every minute. Stir in the raisins, if using. Serve hot with ice cream.

MICROWAVE COURSE GUIDANCE NOTES

If a lining is required for a container use greaseproof paper.

Always cover steamed puddings with a piece of cling film which should fit tightly around the sides of the basin but be slack enough to allow for rising, unless instructions are given to the contrary.

Turn the container around halfway through cooking.

Steamed puddings are best served immediately they are cooked as they tend to harden as they cool.

A very small quantity of water is required when stewing hard fruits, such as apples and plums. A rough guide is 45–60 ml (3–4 tbsp) water to 450 g (1 lb) fruit.

Soft fruits, such as blackberries and raspberries, do not generally require any additional water.

Egg-and-milk-based puddings are more successful if cooked on Defrost.

When cooking individual puddings or fruit, such as baked apples, arrange them in a circle with a space between each. Avoid placing any food in the centre of the ring.

CANNED PUDDING

SERVES ▶ 2
SETTING ▶ HIGH
TIME ▶ 3 MINUTES
GRADING ▶ VERY EASY

300 g (10.6 oz) can sponge pudding
hot Basic Custard, to serve (see page 97)

Remove the pudding from the can and place it on a plate. Cover with cling film, pulling back one corner

to allow steam to escape and cook for 3 minutes or until hot. Serve immediately with hot Basic Custard.

HOT ORANGE RICE

SERVES ▶ 4
SETTING ▶ HIGH
TIME ▶ 4½ MINUTES
GRADING ▶ VERY EASY

439 g (16 oz) can creamed rice
312 g (11 oz) can mandarin oranges, drained
1.25 ml (¼ level tsp) grated nutmeg

1 Stir together the rice and oranges in a 2 litre (3½ pint) bowl. Cook, uncovered, for 4½ minutes or until hot. Stir halfway through cooking.

2 Pour into a warm serving bowl. Sprinkle with grated nutmeg.

———— TIP ————
YOU CAN USE ANY CANNED DRAINED FRUIT INSTEAD OF ORANGES.

RICE PUDDING

SERVES ▶ 4
SETTING ▶ HIGH
TIME ▶ 43 MINUTES
GRADING ▶ EASY

568 ml (1 pint) milk
50 g (2 oz) pudding rice
25 g (1 oz) caster sugar
15 g (½ oz) butter or margarine
2.5 ml (½ level tsp) grated nutmeg

1 Put all the ingredients in a 2.75 litre (4½–5 pint) bowl and cook, uncovered, on High for 8 minutes or until the mixture begins to boil. Stir halfway through cooking.

2 Reduce to Defrost and cook, uncovered, for 35 minutes or until the rice is soft and the pudding creamy. Stir halfway through cooking. Serve hot or cold.

BASIC SPONGE PUDDING

SERVES ▶	4
SETTING ▶	HIGH
TIME ▶	5 MINUTES
GRADING ▶	EASY

100 g (4 oz) butter or margarine

100 g (4 oz) caster sugar

2 eggs, size 2, lightly beaten

100 g (4 oz) self-raising flour

2 drops vanilla flavouring

syrup or jam or Basic Custard (see page 97) or Basic Sweet White Sauce (page 93), to serve

1 Cream together the butter and sugar. Beat in the eggs one at a time, beating well after each addition. Fold in the flour and vanilla flavouring.

2 Spoon the mixture into a greased 900 ml (1½ pint) ovenproof pudding basin. Cover with cling film, pressing it around the sides of the basin and making sure that it is slack in the centre to allow for the pudding to rise. Cook for 5 minutes. Turn around halfway through cooking.

3 Before leaving the pudding to stand, raise the edge of the cling film furthest away from you in order to allow the steam to escape, then leave to stand, covered, for 4 minutes. Loosen the pudding with a knife and turn out. Serve immediately. Serve with syrup or jam, or Basic Custard or Sweet White Sauce, if wished.

BASIC SUET PUDDING

SERVES ▶	4
SETTING ▶	HIGH
TIME ▶	4 MINUTES
GRADING ▶	EASY

100 g (4 oz) self-raising flour

50 g (2 oz) shredded suet

50 g (2 oz) caster sugar

1 egg, size 2, lightly beaten

60 ml (4 tbsp) milk

2 drops vanilla flavouring

Basic Sweet White Sauce, to serve (see page 93)

1 Mix together the flour, suet and sugar. Stir in the egg, 30 ml (2 tbsp) water, milk and vanilla flavouring.

2 Spoon the mixture into a greased 900 ml (1½ pint) ovenproof pudding basin. Cover with cling film, pressing it around the sides of the basin and making sure that it is slack in the centre to allow for the pudding to rise. Cook for 4 minutes. Turn around halfway through cooking.

3 Before leaving the pudding to stand, raise the edge of the cling film furthest away from you to allow steam to escape, then leave the pudding to stand, covered, for 4 minutes. Loosen the pudding with a knife and turn out. Serve immediately. Serve with Sweet White Sauce, hot custard, jam or syrup, if wished.

——— TIP ———

ADD 25–50 g (1–2 oz) OF DRIED FRUIT TO THE MIXTURE AT STEP 1 FOR A FRUIT PUDDING.

CHRISTMAS PUDDING

SERVES ▶	6–8
SETTING ▶	HIGH and DEFROST
TIME ▶	24 MINUTES
GRADING ▶	EASY

75 g (3 oz) shredded suet

75 g (3 oz) plain flour

5 ml (1 level tsp) mixed ground spice

2.5 ml ($\frac{1}{2}$ level tsp) grated nutmeg

2.5 ml ($\frac{1}{2}$ level tsp) ground cinnamon

1.25 ml ($\frac{1}{4}$ level tsp) salt

50 g (2 oz) caster sugar

50 g (2 oz) soft dark brown sugar

40 g (1$\frac{1}{2}$ oz) fresh white breadcrumbs

50 g (2 oz) glacé cherries, quartered

50 g (2 oz) mixed peel

75 g (3 oz) currants

75 g (3 oz) sultanas

75 g (3 oz) stoned dates, chopped

50 g (2 oz) walnuts, chopped

50 g (2 oz) cored, peeled and chopped apple

grated rind and juice of 1 orange

2 eggs, size 2, lightly beaten

25 ml (1 fl oz) milk

25 ml (1 fl oz) brandy

10 ml (2 level tsp) gravy browning

butter or margarine, for greasing

caster sugar, to decorate

Basic Custard, to serve (see page 97)

1 Mix all the dry ingredients together. Stir in the orange rind and juice, the eggs and milk. Mix the brandy and gravy browning together and stir into the pudding.

2 Spoon the mixture into a 1.1 litre (2 pint) pudding basin which has been well greased with butter. Make a small dip in the centre of the pudding. Cover with cling film which should fit snugly around the sides of the bowl but should be slack in the centre to allow for rising. Cook on Defrost for 20 minutes. Turn around halfway through cooking.

3 Before standing, raise one corner of the cling film furthest away from you to allow steam to escape, then leave the pudding to stand, covered, for 5 minutes. Increase the power setting to High. Re-cover and cook for 4 minutes. Before standing, raise the edge of the cling film furthest away from you to allow steam to escape, then stand, covered, for 5 minutes. Loosen the pudding with a knife and turn out on to a warmed serving dish.

4 If wished 15 ml (1 tbsp) of brandy can be warmed conventionally and poured over the pudding once the pudding has been removed from the microwave cooker. The brandy can then be ignited and the pudding served flamed. Alternatively, decorate with a dredging of caster sugar and a holly sprig. Serve with hot Basic Custard.

——— TIPS ———

SILVER CHARMS AND COINS *MUST NOT* BE PUT INTO THE PUDDING BEFORE COOKING.

SHOULD THE PUDDING BE REHEATED, REFER TO THE COOKER MANUFACTURER'S BOOK FOR SPECIFIC INSTRUCTIONS AND *DO NOT* LEAVE THE PUDDING UNATTENDED.

UNLIKE TRADITIONAL CHRISTMAS PUDDING, THIS PUDDING IS NOT SUITABLE FOR LENGTHY STORAGE.

SUMMER PUDDING

SERVES ▶ 4–6
SETTING ▶ HIGH
TIME ▶ 7 MINUTES
GRADING ▶ LESS EASY

225 g (8 oz) blackcurrants, stringed

225 g (8 oz) raspberries

225 g (8 oz) strawberries, hulled

100 g (4 oz) caster sugar

9–10 slices of white bread, 0.5 cm ($\frac{1}{4}$ inch) thick, with crusts removed

45 ml (3 tbsp) brandy (optional)

fresh blackcurrants, raspberries and strawberries, to decorate

300 ml ($\frac{1}{2}$ pint) double cream, to serve

1 Stir together the blackcurrants, raspberries, strawberries and caster sugar in a 2 litre ($3\frac{1}{2}$ pint) bowl. Cover with cling film, pulling back one corner to allow steam to escape and cook for 7 minutes or until blackcurrants are cooked. Stir halfway through cooking.

2 Line the base and sides of a 1.1 litre (2 pint) pudding basin with the bread, ensuring that the slices overlap. Reserve enough for the top.

3 Spoon the fruit into the basin and sprinkle over 30 ml (2 tbsp) of brandy, if using. Cover with the remaining slices of bread. Spoon over some of the juice to colour the bread. Reserve the juice. Put a saucer or small plate on top of the pudding and place a weight on top of this. Refrigerate the pudding for 24 hours.

4 Carefully turn out the pudding on to a serving dish. Stir 15 ml (1 tbsp) brandy, if using, into the reserved juice and spoon over the pudding, ensuring that all the bread is evenly covered. Decorate the pudding with the fresh fruit and serve with the cream.

HOT CHOCOLATE PUDDING

SERVES ▶ 4
SETTING ▶ HIGH and DEFROST
TIME ▶ 13 MINUTES
GRADING ▶ EASY

100 g (4 oz) plain chocolate, broken into pieces

50 g (2 oz) butter or margarine, cut into pieces

300 ml ($\frac{1}{2}$ pint) milk

30 ml (2 tbsp) sweet sherry

50 g (2 oz) soft dark brown sugar

1.25 ml ($\frac{1}{4}$ tsp) vanilla flavouring

2 eggs, size 2, separated

150 g (5 oz) fresh white breadcrumbs

150 ml ($\frac{1}{4}$ pint) double cream

50 g (2 oz) plain chocolate, grated, to decorate

1 Put the chocolate pieces in a 600 ml (1 pint) jug. Cook, uncovered, for 2 minutes or until melted. Stir frequently after 1 minute. Stir in the butter until melted. Set aside.

2 Put the milk in a 600 ml (1 pint) jug. Cook, uncovered, for 3 minutes. Beat the milk into the chocolate. Beat in the sherry, sugar, vanilla flavouring and egg yolks. Finally, beat in the breadcrumbs.

3 Whisk the egg whites until stiff peaks form, then fold them into the mixture. Pour into a 900 ml ($1\frac{1}{2}$ pint) ovenproof dish. Cook, uncovered, for 4 minutes. Gently stir after 2 minutes and 4 minutes.

4 Reduce to Defrost and cook, uncovered, for 4 minutes. Pour the double cream over the top. Stand for 3–4 minutes. Decorate with grated chocolate.

HOT DATE PUDDING

SERVES ▶ 4
SETTING ▶ HIGH
TIME ▶ 5 MINUTES
GRADING ▶ EASY

100 g (4 oz) butter or margarine

100 g (4 oz) caster sugar

2 eggs, size 2

175 g (6 oz) self-raising flour

30 ml (2 tbsp) milk

75 g (3 oz) stoned dates, chopped

caster sugar, to decorate

cream or Basic Custard, to serve (see page 97)

1 Beat together the butter and sugar until light and fluffy. Beat in the eggs, one at a time, beating well after each addition.

2 Fold in the flour. Gently stir in the milk and dates. Spoon the mixture into a 1.1 litre (2 pint) greased pudding basin. Cover with cling film which fits tightly around the sides of the basin but is slack in the centre to allow for rising and cook for 5 minutes. Turn around halfway through cooking.

3 Before standing, raise one corner of the cling film furthest away from you to allow steam to escape, then stand, covered, for 2 minutes. Turn out on to a warmed serving dish. Decorate the top with sprinkled caster sugar. Serve with cream or Custard.

CHERRIES WITH CREAM

SERVES ▶ 4
SETTING ▶ HIGH
TIME ▶ 4½ MINUTES
GRADING ▶ EASY

700 g (1½ lb) black cherries, with stalks removed and stoned

15 ml (1 level tbsp) caster sugar

10 ml (2 level tsp) gelatine

few drops red food colouring

150 ml (¼ pint) double cream

cherries with stalks and 150 ml (¼ pint) whipping cream, to decorate

1 Put the cherries and sugar in a 2 litre (3½ pint) bowl. Cover with cling film, pulling back one corner to allow steam to escape and cook for 4½ minutes or until cherries are cooked. Stir halfway through cooking.

2 Put the cherries in a blender or food processor, sprinkle in the gelatine. Blend until smooth. Add the red food colouring. Pour into a bowl. Set aside to cool for about 20 minutes.

3 Whisk the double cream until stiff peaks form, then gently fold it into the purée. Pour into 4 dishes and chill. Whisk the whipping cream and decorate the dishes with the cream and cherries.

RUM CHOCOLATE MOUSSE

SERVES ▶	4
SETTING ▶	HIGH
TIME ▶	2 MINUTES
GRADING ▶	EASY

225 g (8 oz) plain chocolate, broken into pieces

25 g (1 oz) butter or margarine

30 ml (2 tbsp) dark rum

4 eggs, size 2, separated

150 ml (¼ pint) double cream and chocolate curls, to decorate

1 Put the chocolate in a 2 litre (3½ pint) bowl. Cook, uncovered, for 2 minutes or until melted. Stir frequently after 1 minute. Beat in the butter, rum and egg yolks.

2 Whisk the egg whites until stiff peaks form, then gently fold them into the rum and chocolate mixture. Spoon the mixture into 4 glasses and put in the refrigerator to chill. Whip the cream until stiff and decorate the mousses with cream chocolate curls. Serve with langue de chat biscuits, if wished.

PEACHES AND COCONUT PURÉE

SERVES ▶	4
SETTING ▶	HIGH
TIME ▶	7 MINUTES
GRADING ▶	EASY

550 g (1¼ lb) peaches, stoned and quartered

15 ml (1 tbsp) sweet sherry

25 g (1 oz) caster sugar

40 g (1½ oz) desiccated coconut

15 ml (3 level tsp) gelatine

150 ml (¼ pint) double cream

whipped cream and toasted desiccated coconut, to decorate

1 Put the peaches, sherry, 30 ml (2 tbsp) water, sugar and coconut in a 2 litre (3½ pint) bowl. Cover with cling film, pulling back one corner to allow steam to escape and cook for 7 minutes or until tender. Stir halfway through cooking.

2 Pour the mixture into a blender or a food processor. Sprinkle in the gelatine and blend until the gelatine has dissolved. Set aside to cool for about 45 minutes.

3 Whisk the cream until stiff and gently fold it into the purée. Pour into 4 large wine glasses. Refrigerate to chill. Whip the cream and decorate the purée with rosettes of cream and toasted coconut.

ORANGE **S**PONGE
PUDDINGS

SERVES ▶ 4	
SETTING ▶ HIGH	
TIME ▶ 4 MINUTES	
GRADING ▶ EASY	

50 g (2 oz) butter or margarine

50 g (2 oz) caster sugar

1 egg, size 2, lightly beaten

75 g (3 oz) self-raising flour

15 ml (1 tbsp) milk

grated rind of 1 orange

2 drops vanilla flavouring

45 ml (3 level tbsp) marmalade

*Marmalade Sauce (see page 98) or Basic
   Custard, to serve (see page 97)*

1 Cream the butter and sugar together. Beat in the
   egg. Fold in the flour, milk, orange rind and
vanilla flavouring.

2 Spread the marmalade over the base of 4
   greased 150 ml ($\frac{1}{4}$ pint) ramekin dishes or 4
drinking mugs. Cook, uncovered, for 1 minute.

3 Divide and spoon the sponge mixture over the
   marmalade. Cover with cling film, which should
be tight around the sides but slack in the middle to
allow for rising. Arrange in a circle on the floor of
the cooker and cook for 3 minutes or until cooked
through. Reposition halfway through cooking.

4 Loosen the edges with a knife. Turn out on to
   warmed serving dishes. Serve with Marmalade
Sauce or Basic Custard.

SYRUP **T**ART

SERVES ▶ 4–6	
SETTING ▶ HIGH	
TIME ▶ 8$\frac{1}{2}$ MINUTES	
GRADING ▶ LESS EASY	

175 g (6 oz) plain flour

pinch of salt

40 g (1$\frac{1}{2}$ oz) butter or margarine

40 g (1$\frac{1}{2}$ oz) lard

10 ml (2 level tsp) ground cinnamon

225 ml (8 fl oz) golden syrup

90 g (3$\frac{1}{2}$ oz) fresh white breadcrumbs

grated rind and juice of 1 lemon

Basic Custard, to serve (see page 97)

1 Put the flour and salt in a bowl. Rub in the
   butter and lard until the mixture resembles fine
breadcrumbs. Add sufficient water to form a firm
dough.

2 Roll out the dough and sprinkle with cinnamon.
   Rub it lightly over the pastry with the fingertips.
Use to line a 15 cm (6 inch) ovenproof glass pie
plate. Prick the base and sides thoroughly. Cook,
uncovered, for 3$\frac{1}{2}$ minutes or until crisp. Set aside.

3 Put the syrup, breadcrumbs and lemon rind and
   juice in a 1 litre (1$\frac{3}{4}$ pint) jug. Cook, uncovered,
for 2 minutes.

4 Pour the syrup mixture into the flan case. Cook,
   uncovered, for 3 minutes. Serve hot or cold.

——————— TIP ———————

ROLL OUT THE SCRAPS OF PASTRY AND CUT INTO CIRCLES
WITH A SMALL FANCY CUTTER. PLACE ON A PIECE OF
GREASEPROOF PAPER. COOK, UNCOVERED, FOR 1 MINUTE OR
UNTIL THE PASTRY IS CRISP. USE TO DECORATE THE TART.
SERVE WITH HOT CUSTARD OR ICE CREAM, IF WISHED.

CHOCOLATE CUSTARD PIE

SERVES ▶	4–6
SETTING ▶	HIGH
TIME ▶	$4\frac{3}{4}$ MINUTES
GRADING ▶	LESS EASY

75 g (3 oz) butter or margarine

175 g (6 oz) digestive biscuits, crushed

65 g (2½ oz) caster sugar

25 g (1 oz) cornflour

25 g (1 oz) cocoa powder

150 ml (¼ pint) evaporated milk

300 ml (½ pint) milk

150 ml (¼ pint) double cream and chocolate buttons, to decorate

1 Put 50 g (2 oz) of the butter in a 600 ml (1 pint) jug. Cook, uncovered, for 45 seconds or until melted. Stir the butter into the biscuits and add 25 g (1 oz) of the caster sugar. Using the back of a spoon, press the mixture over the base and sides of an 18 cm (7 inch) flan dish.

2 Put the cornflour, remaining 40 g (1½ oz) caster sugar and the cocoa powder in a 1 litre (1¾ pint) jug. Gradually blend in the evaporated milk and fresh milk. Cook, uncovered, for 4 minutes. Stir every minute.

3 Beat in the remaining 25 g (1 oz) butter. Pour the mixture into the flan case. Set aside until cold, then chill.

4 Whisk the cream until stiff, then decorate the pie with the cream and chocolate buttons.

——— TIPS ———

USE CHOCOLATE POWDER INSTEAD OF COCOA POWDER BUT ADJUST THE SUGAR TO TASTE AS CHOCOLATE POWDER IS ALREADY SWEETENED.

USE ALL FRESH MILK INSTEAD OF EVAPORATED AND FRESH MILK, IF WISHED.

CHILLED STRAWBERRY SEMOLINA

SERVES ▶	4
SETTING ▶	HIGH
TIME ▶	$7–7\frac{1}{2}$ MINUTES
GRADING ▶	EASY

45 ml (3 tbsp) orange juice

50 g (2 oz) caster sugar

45 ml (3 level tbsp) semolina

2 egg whites, size 2

60 ml (4 level tbsp) strawberry jam, sieved

1 Put the orange juice and 300 ml (½ pint) water into a 1 litre (1¾ pint) jug. Cook, uncovered, for 3½ minutes.

2 Stir in the sugar and semolina. Cook, uncovered, for 2½ minutes. Stir every minute. Set aside to cool for about 45 minutes. Stir occasionally.

3 Whisk the egg whites until stiff. Fold into the semolina and divide among 4 glass dishes. Chill.

4 Put 30 ml (2 tbsp) water and the jam in a 600 ml (1 pint) jug. Cook, uncovered, for 1–1½ minutes. Stir well. Cool for about 10 minutes. Pour the jam over the semolina in the glasses. Allow to chill.

——— TIP ———

ANY FLAVOUR OF JAM CAN BE CHOSEN TO GO WITH THE SEMOLINA.

ORANGE COFFEE DESSERT

SERVES ▶ 4	
SETTING ▶ HIGH	
TIME ▶ 3 MINUTES	
GRADING ▶ EASY	

150 ml ($\frac{1}{4}$ pint) orange juice

15 ml (3 tsp) coffee essence

15 ml (3 level tsp) gelatine

grated rind of 1 orange

2 eggs, size 2, separated

50 g (2 oz) caster sugar

450 ml ($\frac{3}{4}$ pint) whipping cream

pared orange rind, to decorate

1 Put the orange juice and coffee essence in a 600 ml (1 pint) jug. Cook, uncovered, for 2 minutes. Sprinkle in the gelatine and stir until dissolved. Set aside to cool, for about 15 minutes. Stir in the orange rind.

2 Put the egg yolks and sugar in a 1 litre (1$\frac{3}{4}$ pint) jug. Beat together. Cook, uncovered, for 30 seconds. Using an electric mixer beat for 30 seconds. Cook, uncovered, for a further 30 seconds. Continue beating until thick and creamy. Set aside.

3 Whisk the cream until stiff. Whisk the egg whites until stiff.

4 Stir the orange mixture into the egg yolk mixture. Transfer to a 2 litre (3$\frac{1}{2}$ pint) bowl. Fold two-thirds of the cream and the egg whites into the mixture.

5 Pour the mixture into 4 glass dishes. Refrigerate until set. Decorate the dessert with the remaining whipped cream and orange rind.

——— TIP ———
INSTANT COFFEE OR FRESHLY-MADE COFFEE CAN BE USED INSTEAD OF COFFEE ESSENCE, IF WISHED.

CHOCOLATE MINT ICE CREAM

SERVES ▶ 4–6	
SETTING ▶ HIGH	
TIME ▶ 2$\frac{1}{2}$ MINUTES	
GRADING ▶ EASY	

150 g (5 oz) mint chip chocolates

4 eggs, size 2, separated

300 ml ($\frac{1}{2}$ pint) double cream

100 g (4 oz) caster sugar

1 Put the chocolate in a 1 litre (1$\frac{3}{4}$ pint) jug. Cook, uncovered, for 2 minutes or until it is melted. Stir frequently after 1 minute. Cool slightly, then beat in the egg yolks. Set aside.

2 Whisk the cream until stiff. Whisk into the chocolate.

3 Whisk the egg whites until stiff. Whisk in the sugar 1 teaspoonful at a time, then fold into the chocolate mixture. Set aside.

4 Pour into a 1.7 litre (3 pint) container. Freeze until frozen. (Stirring during freezing is not necessary.) Remove from the freezer and transfer to the refrigerator for 10–15 minutes to soften slightly before serving.

PINEAPPLE SORBET

SERVES ▶ 6
SETTING ▶ HIGH
TIME ▶ $3\frac{1}{2}$ MINUTES
GRADING ▶ LESS EASY

1 ripe fresh pineapple, weighing 900 g–1.4 kg (2–3 lb), cut in half and the flesh removed (saving the pineapple shells, for serving if wished)

100 g (4 oz) granulated sugar

15 ml (3 level tsp) gelatine

45 ml (3 tbsp) orange juice

2 egg whites, size 2

1 In a blender or food processor, purée the pineapple flesh. Make up to 900 ml ($1\frac{1}{2}$ pints) with cold water.

2 Put 300 ml ($\frac{1}{2}$ pint) fruit purée into a 1 litre ($1\frac{3}{4}$ pint) jug. Stir in the sugar and gelatine. Cook, uncovered, for $3\frac{1}{2}$ minutes. Stir halfway through cooking. Stir well to dissolve the sugar.

3 Stir in the remaining purée and orange juice. Set aside to cool for about 20 minutes. Pour into a shallow container and freeze until the edges of the mixture begin to set.

4 Turn the mixture into a bowl. Whisk until thick. Whisk the egg whites until stiff and fold into the purée mixture.

5 Pour into a container or, if desired, the half pineapple shells. Freeze until frozen.

6 Remove from the freezer and transfer to the refrigerator for 15 minutes to soften slightly before serving.

CHERRY WATER ICE

SERVES ▶ 4
SETTING ▶ HIGH
TIME ▶ 5 MINUTES
GRADING ▶ EASY

175 g (6 oz) granulated sugar

450 g (1 lb) cherries, stalks removed and stoned

cherries with stalks, to decorate

1 Put the sugar and 300 ml ($\frac{1}{2}$ pint) water in a 1 litre ($1\frac{3}{4}$ pint) jug. Cook, uncovered, for 5 minutes. Stir halfway through cooking. Stir well to dissolve the sugar.

2 Liquidise the cherries in a blender or food processor, and stir into the sugar water liquid. Cool for about 15 minutes. Pour into a shallow container and freeze until the edges of the mixture begin to freeze.

3 Turn the mixture into a bowl. Whisk well and return to the container. Freeze until frozen.

4 Remove from the freezer and transfer to the refrigerator for 10 minutes to soften slightly before serving. Decorate with fresh cherries.

——— TIP ———

USE PLUMS INSTEAD OF CHERRIES, IF WISHED.

RUM AND **R**AISIN **I**CE **C**REAM

SERVES ▶ 4–6
SETTING ▶ HIGH
TIME ▶ 7 MINUTES
GRADING ▶ EASY

300 ml ($\frac{1}{2}$ pint) milk

1 egg, size 2, plus 2 egg yolks

15 ml (1 tbsp) rum

450 ml ($\frac{3}{4}$ pint) double cream

50 g (2 oz) raisins

raisins, to decorate

1 Put the milk in a 600 ml (1 pint) jug. Cook, uncovered, for 3 minutes or until boiling. Set aside for 10 minutes.

2 Beat the egg and egg yolks until pale and creamy. Stir in the milk and rum. Strain into a 1 litre (1$\frac{3}{4}$ pint) jug. Cook, uncovered, for 4 minutes. Whisk briskly every minute to avoid curdling. Whisk well before setting aside to cool for about 15 minutes, whisking occasionally.

3 Whisk the cream until stiff. Gently fold two-thirds of the cream into the cooled egg custard. Pour into a shallow container and freeze until partially frozen. Cover remaining cream and refrigerate.

4 Transfer the ice cream to a bowl and whisk until smooth. Stir in the raisins. Pour into a 600 ml (1 pint) ice cream bombe. Freeze until frozen.

5 Remove from freezer 10–15 minutes before required and transfer to the refrigerator, to soften slightly. Turn out on to a chilled serving plate. Decorate the ice cream with the remaining cream and raisins.

LEMON **C**URD **C**HEESECAKE

SERVES ▶ 6–8
SETTING ▶ HIGH
TIME ▶ 6$\frac{1}{2}$ MINUTES
GRADING ▶ LESS EASY

15 ml (1 tbsp) golden syrup

100 g (4 oz) butter or margarine

225 g (8 oz) digestive biscuits, crushed

175 g (6 oz) curd cheese

175 g (6 oz) full fat soft cheese

30 ml (2 level tbsp) lemon curd

15 ml (1 level tbsp) caster sugar

2 eggs, size 2, lightly beaten

grated rind of 1 lemon

100 g (4 oz) sultanas

pared lemon rind

pared lemon rind, to decorate

1 Put the syrup and butter in a 2 litre (3$\frac{1}{2}$ pint) bowl. Cook, uncovered, for 1$\frac{1}{2}$ minutes or until melted. Stir in the biscuits. Sprinkle the mixture into a 20.5 cm (8 inch) loose based sandwich tin. Press the mixture over the base and sides with the back of a spoon. Set aside.

2 Put the curd cheese, full fat cheese, lemon curd, sugar, eggs and lemon rind into a 2 litre (3$\frac{1}{2}$ pint) bowl. Beat together.

3 Cook, uncovered, for 5 minutes. Beat well after 2 minutes and 4 minutes. After cooking, beat well until smooth.

4 Stir in the sultanas. Spoon the mixture into the flan case. Cool and chill.

5 Remove the flan from the tin. Decorate with strips of lemon rind.

ORANGE SORBET

SERVES ▶ 6	
SETTING ▶ HIGH	
TIME ▶ 4 MINUTES	
GRADING ▶ EASY	

900 ml (1½ pints) orange juice

grated rind of 2 oranges

15 ml (3 level tsp) gelatine

150 g (5 oz) granulated sugar

2 egg whites, size 2

1 Put 300 ml (½ pint) orange juice into a 1 litre (1¾ pint) jug. Stir in the rind, gelatine and sugar. Cook, uncovered, for 4 minutes. Stir halfway through cooking. Stir well to dissolve the sugar.

2 Stir in the remaining orange juice. Set aside to cool for about 15 minutes. Pour into a shallow container and freeze until the edges of the mixture begin to set.

3 Turn the mixture into a bowl. Whisk until thick. Whisk the egg whites until stiff and fold into the orange mixture.

4 Pour into a large container and freeze until frozen. Remove from the freezer and transfer to the refrigerator for 15 minutes to soften slightly before serving.

——— TIP ———
USE ANY FRUIT JUICE OF YOUR CHOICE TO FLAVOUR THIS SORBET.

CARIBBEAN BANANAS

SERVES ▶ 4	
SETTING ▶ HIGH	
TIME ▶ 6 MINUTES	
GRADING ▶ LESS EASY	

25 g (1 oz) butter or margarine

50 g (2 oz) soft dark brown sugar

4 large bananas, peeled and halved

60 ml (4 tbsp) dark rum

1 Put the butter in a shallow dish and cook uncovered for 45 seconds, or until melted. Add the sugar and cook uncovered for 1 minute. Stir until the sugar has dissolved. Add the bananas and coat with the sugar mixture. Cook uncovered for 4 minutes, turning the fruit over once.

2 Put the rum in a cup and cook uncovered for 30 seconds, pour over the bananas and flambé immediately. Serve at once with cream.

Opposite
*C*hocolate *C*oconut *B*alls (page 124), *W*hite *D*ates (page 124), *O*range *C*offee *F*udge (page 125)

C O O K W A R E
~à la~
M I C R O W A V E

■ Take one Corning covered browning casserole. ■ Add a larg[e]
Corning oval dish and a Corning divided oval dish. ■ Mix togethe[r]
with the Corning round casserole and Corning serving dish, graduall[y]
blending in a Corning round shallow dish. ■ Sprinkle liberally wit[h]
Vision browning dishes and casseroles. ■ Heat in the oven or on th[e]
hob and serve at the table. (Or alternatively, freeze till later.) ■

CAKES AND **B**ISCUITS

MICROWAVE COURSE GUIDANCE NOTES

Cakes cooked in a microwave cooker will lack the colour and texture of cakes cooked conventionally.

If a lining is required use greaseproof paper.

Cakes and biscuits should not be covered unless instructions are given to the contrary.

If extra liquid is required, milk will often extend the keeping qualities of the cakes or biscuits.

Turn the container around at least once during cooking.

Remove cakes from the cooker when they have a little moisture on the top. This prevents overcooking.

Raise fruit and large cake containers on a trivet or upturned pie plate during cooking so that the microwaves can penetrate the cake on all sides.

Decorate cakes upside down so that the smoother surface is uppermost.

If cooking individual cakes and biscuits arrange them in a circle with a space between each. Do not put a cake in the centre.

To avoid small paper cases collapsing stand them in ramekin dishes.

CHOCOLATE CAKE

SERVES ▶	6–8
SETTING ▶	HIGH
TIME ▶	8 MINUTES
GRADING ▶	EASY

175 g (6 oz) butter or soft margarine

175 g (6 oz) caster sugar

1.25 ml ($\frac{1}{4}$ tsp) vanilla flavouring

45 ml (3 tbsp) milk

3 eggs, size 2

150 g (5 oz) self-raising flour

5 ml (1 level tsp) baking powder

40 g ($1\frac{1}{2}$ oz) cocoa powder

175 g (6 oz) butter or margarine

350 g (12 oz) icing sugar, sieved

20 ml (4 level tsp) cocoa powder, sieved

20 ml (4 tsp) orange juice

75 g (3 oz) chocolate vermicelli

1 Grease an 18 cm (7 inch) round, 9 cm ($3\frac{1}{2}$ inch) deep container and line the base with greaseproof paper.

2 Put the butter, caster sugar, vanilla flavouring, milk and eggs in a large bowl. Sift in the flour, baking powder and cocoa powder. Beat until the mixture is smooth but do not over-beat.

3 Spoon the mixture into the prepared container and spread evenly. Stand on a trivet or up-turned pie plate. Cook for 8 minutes or until risen but still looks slightly moist on the surface. Turn the container once during cooking.

4 Leave the cake to stand for 5 minutes before turning out on to a greaseproof paper-covered wire rack to cool. Cut the cake in half.

5 To make the icing, cream the butter until light and fluffy, beat in the icing sugar and cocoa powder. Gradually beat in the orange juice until the butter icing is soft and smooth.

6 Using a hot dry palette knife sandwich the cake together with a little of the icing. Spread the remaining icing over the sides and top of the cake. Coat the sides and top with vermicelli.

COCONUT BANANA RING

SERVES ▶	6–8
SETTING ▶	HIGH
TIME ▶	8 MINUTES
GRADING ▶	EASY

2 eggs, size 2

60 ml (4 tbsp) milk

150 g (5 oz) soft dark brown sugar

100 g (4 oz) butter or soft margarine

450 g (1 lb) bananas, peeled and chopped

225 g (8 oz) self-raising flour

1.25 ml ($\frac{1}{4}$ level tsp) baking powder

40 g ($1\frac{1}{2}$ oz) desiccated coconut

for the topping
75 g (3 oz) icing sugar, sieved

15 g ($\frac{1}{2}$ oz) desiccated coconut, toasted

1 Grease a 2.3 litre (4 pint) microwave ring mould.

2 Blend the eggs, milk, sugar, butter and bananas in a blender or food processor until smooth. Sift the flour and baking powder into a bowl and stir in the desiccated coconut and banana mixture.

3 Spread and spoon the mixture evenly in the prepared mould. Cook, uncovered, for 8 minutes or until risen but still looks slightly moist on the surface. Turn round once during cooking. Stand for 5 minutes before turning out on to a wire cooling rack covered with greaseproof paper. Leave to cool.

4 For the topping, beat together the icing sugar and 10 ml (2 tsp) warm water. The icing should be thick enough to coat the back of a spoon. Add a little yellow colouring. Pour the icing over the top of the ring. Sprinkle with toasted coconut.

FLORENTINES

SERVES ▶ 16 BISCUITS	
SETTING ▶ HIGH	
TIME ▶ 8–9¾ MINUTES	
GRADING ▶ EASY	

50 g (2 oz) butter or margarine

15 ml (1 tbsp) golden syrup

50 g (2 oz) soft dark brown sugar

25 g (1 oz) plain flour

1.25 ml (¼ level tsp) ground cinnamon

15 g (½ oz) angelica, chopped

75 g (3 oz) chopped mixed nuts

50 g (2 oz) glacé cherries, chopped

25 g (1 oz) sultanas

75 g (3 oz) plain chocolate, broken into pieces

1 Put the butter in a 2 litre (3½ pint) bowl. Cook, uncovered, for 45 seconds or until melted. Stir in the syrup and sugar.

2 Beat in the flour and cinnamon. Stir in the angelica, nuts, cherries and sultanas. Using 2 teaspoons, put 4 rounds of mixture, spread apart, in a circle on a piece of greaseproof paper. Cook, uncovered, for 1½–1¾ minutes or until set.

3 Remove the biscuits and greaseproof paper from the cooker and using a knife, neaten the edges. Leave on the paper until cool enough to transfer to a wire cooling rack. Repeat this process until all the mixture is used.

4 Put the chocolate in a 600 ml (1 pint) jug. Cook for 2 minutes or until melted. Stir frequently after 1 minute. Using a teaspoon spread the chocolate over the centre of each biscuit.

FUDGE FINGERS

MAKES ▶ 14 FINGERS	
SETTING ▶ HIGH	
TIME ▶ 3½ MINUTES	
GRADING ▶ EASY	

175 g (6 oz) milk chocolate, broken into pieces

75 ml (5 tbsp) condensed milk

10 ml (2 level tsp) cocoa powder

2.5 ml (½ tsp) rum flavouring

225 g (8 oz) shortbread biscuits, crushed

50 g (2 oz) raisins

50 g (2 oz) stoned dates, chopped

25 g (1 oz) peanuts, chopped

1 Grease a 20 cm (8 inch) square cake tin.

2 Put the chocolate in a 2 litre (3½ pint) bowl. Cook, uncovered, for 2 minutes or until melted. Stir frequently after 1 minute. Stir in the condensed milk, cocoa powder and rum flavouring. Cook, uncovered, for 1½ minutes.

3 Stir the biscuits, raisins, dates and nuts into the milk mixture. Spread in the prepared container and smooth over the top with the back of a hot, damp tablespoon.

4 Refrigerate until set. Cut into 14 fingers, to serve.

PRESERVES

MICROWAVE COURSE GUIDANCE NOTES

Use the conventional method for preserving jams if a yield of more than 1.1 kg (2½ lb) is required.

Always use a very large container, at least 2.75 litre (4½–5 pint), to avoid boiling over.

Use a container made of a meterial which withstands the high temperatures of boiling sugar.

Never cover the container when cooking preserves unless instructions are given to the contrary.

Never leave a thermometer in the container during cooking.

'Mushy' chutneys are not easily made in a microwave cooker.

Less liquid may be required when cooking chutney because there is less evaporation.

It is not advisable to bottle fruit or vegetables in a microwave cooker.

Fruit skins such as lemon, orange and grapefruit tend to remain firm when cooked. For more tender skins, grate or chop finely the rind before using.

Fruit with skins such as gooseberries may be less soft than when cooked by the conventional method.

PLUM **J**AM

MAKES ▶ 900 g (2 lb)
SETTING ▶ HIGH
TIME ▶ 24–27 MINUTES
GRADING ▶ LESS EASY

700 g (1½ lb) plums, quartered and stones removed

450 g (1 lb) granulated sugar

1 Put the plums in a 2.75 litre (4½–5 pint) bowl. Cover with cling film, pulling back one corner to allow steam to escape and cook for 7 minutes.

2 Stir in the sugar until dissolved. Cook, un-covered, for 17–20 minutes or until setting point is reached. Stir twice during cooking.

3 To test for setting, put 15 ml (1 tbsp) of jam on a cold saucer and allow to cool. Push the edge of the jam with a finger. If the jam wrinkles or frills then setting point has been reached.

4 Stand, uncovered, for 10 minutes. Spoon into two 450 g (1 lb) warm, sterilised jars. Place a wax disc over the jam, cover and label.

DRIED **A**PRICOT **J**AM WITH **A**LMONDS

MAKES ▶ ABOUT 900 g (2 lb)
SETTING ▶ HIGH
TIME ▶ ABOUT 45 MINUTES
GRADING ▶ LESS EASY

225 g (8 oz) dried apricots, coarsely chopped

700 g (1½ lb) granulated sugar

25 g (1 oz) split almonds

1 Put the apricots and 750 ml (1¼ pints) cold water in a 2.75 litre (4½–5 pint) bowl and leave to soak overnight.

2 The next day, cover with cling film, pulling back one corner to allow steam to escape and cook for 10 minutes.

3 Stir in the sugar until nearly dissolved. Cook, uncovered, for 35 minutes or until setting point is reached. Stir halfway through cooking. Stir in the almonds.

4 To test for setting, put 15 ml (1 tbsp) of jam on a cold saucer and allow to cool. Push the edge of the jam with a finger. If the jam wrinkles or frills then setting point has been reached.

5 Stand, uncovered, for 10 minutes. Spoon into two 450 g (1 lb) warm sterilised jars. Place a waxed disc over the jam, cover and label.

MARROW JAM

MAKES ▶ ABOUT 900 g (2 lb)	
SETTING ▶ HIGH	
TIME ▶ ABOUT 43 MINUTES	
GRADING ▶ LESS EASY	

700 g (1½ lb) prepared marrow, diced

grated rind and juice of 1½ lemons

800 g (1¾ lb) granulated sugar

2.5 ml (½ level tsp) ground ginger

1 Put the marrow in a 2.75 litre (4½–5 pint) bowl. Cover with cling film, pulling back one corner to allow steam to escape and cook for 12 minutes. Stir halfway through cooking.

2 Stir in the lemon rind, juice and sugar. Cover and leave for 24 hours.

3 Stir in the ground ginger. Cover with cling film, pulling back one corner to allow steam to escape and cook for 10 minutes. Stir halfway through cooking. Remove the cling film, stir to ensure the sugar has dissolved. Continue cooking, uncovered, for 21 minutes or until the marrow is transparent and the syrup is thick. Stir halfway through cooking.

4 Stand, uncovered, for 10 minutes. Spoon into two 450 g (1 lb) warm sterilised jars. Place a wax disc over the jam, cover and label.

RHUBARB CONSERVE

MAKES ▶ ABOUT 900 g (2 lb)	
SETTING ▶ HIGH	
TIME ▶ ABOUT 30 MINUTES	
GRADING ▶ LESS EASY	

700 g (1½ lb) rhubarb, cut into small pieces

1 large orange, peeled, seeded and chopped

700 g (1½ lb) granulated sugar

1 Mix together the rhubarb and orange flesh in a 2.75 litre (4½–5 pint) bowl. Cover with cling film, pulling back one corner to allow steam to escape and cook for 5 minutes. Stir halfway through cooking.

2 Stir in the sugar. Cook, uncovered, for 25 minutes. Stir halfway through cooking.

3 Stand, uncovered, for 10 minutes. Spoon into two 450 g (1 lb) sterilised warm jars. Place a waxed disc over the jam, cover and label.

REDCURRANT JAM

MAKES ▶ ABOUT 450 g (1 lb)	
SETTING ▶ HIGH	
TIME ▶ 20–23 MINUTES	
GRADING ▶ LESS EASY	

450 g (1 lb) redcurrants, stripped off their stalks

350 g (12 oz) granulated sugar

1 Put the redcurrants and sugar in a 2.75 litre ($4\frac{1}{2}$–5 pint) bowl. Cover with cling film, pulling back one corner to allow steam to escape and cook for 8 minutes.

2 Stir well and cook, uncovered, for 12–15 minutes or until setting point is reached. Stir once during cooking.

3 To test for setting, put 15 ml (1 tbsp) of jam on a cold saucer and allow to cool. Push the edge of the jam with a finger. If the jam wrinkles or frills then setting point has been reached.

4 Stand, uncovered, for 10 minutes. Spoon into a 450 g (1 lb) warm sterilised jar. Place a wax disc over the jam, cover and label.

ORANGE CURD

MAKES ▶ 700 g ($1\frac{1}{2}$ lb)	
SETTING ▶ HIGH	
TIME ▶ 9–11 MINUTES	
GRADING ▶ LESS EASY	

150 g (5 oz) butter or margarine, cut into pieces

grated rind and juice of 3 large oranges

grated rind and juice of 1 lemon

225 g (8 oz) caster sugar

5 eggs, size 2, lightly beaten

1 Put the butter, orange rind, juices and sugar in a 2.75 litre ($4\frac{1}{2}$–5 pint) bowl. Cook, uncovered, for 2–3 minutes until the butter has melted.

2 Whisk the eggs into the butter mixture. Cook, uncovered, for 7–8 minutes until the curd is thick. Whisk every minute to prevent curdling.

3 Strain into two 350 g (12 oz) sterilised warm jars. Place a waxed disc over the curd, then cover and label.

——————TIP——————

ORANGE CURD KEEPS FOR 3 WEEKS IN A REFRIGERATOR.

BEETROOT CHUTNEY

MAKES ▶ ABOUT 900 g (2 lb)	
SETTING ▶ HIGH	
TIME ▶ 17 MINUTES	
GRADING ▶ EASY	

350 g (12 oz) cooked beetroot, skinned

225 g (8 oz) cooking apples, peeled and cored

1 medium onion, skinned

50 g (2 oz) soft dark brown sugar

1.25 ml ($\frac{1}{4}$ level tsp) ground ginger

5 ml (1 level tsp) salt

150 ml ($\frac{1}{4}$ pint) wine vinegar

juice of $\frac{1}{2}$ lemon

1 Mince together the beetroot, apples and onion. Put in a 2.75 litre ($4\frac{1}{2}$–5 pint) bowl. Stir in the sugar, ginger and salt. Cook, uncovered, for 9 minutes. Stir halfway through cooking.

2 Stir in the wine vinegar and lemon juice. Cook, uncovered, for 8 minutes. Stir halfway through cooking.

3 Spoon into two 450 g (1 lb) warm sterilised jars. Cover immediately with airtight and vinegar-proof tops. Label and leave to cool.

DATE CHUTNEY

MAKES ▶ ABOUT 1.4 kg (3 lb)	
SETTING ▶ HIGH	
TIME ▶ ABOUT 35 MINUTES	
GRADING ▶ EASY	

350 g (12 oz) tomatoes, roughly chopped

350 g (12 oz) cooking apples, peeled, cored and chopped

1 medium onion, skinned and chopped

350 g (12 oz) stoned dates, chopped

2.5 ml ($\frac{1}{2}$ level tsp) ground ginger

2.5 ml ($\frac{1}{2}$ level tsp) ground cloves

2.5 ml ($\frac{1}{2}$ level tsp) ground mixed spice

1 garlic clove, skinned and crushed

225 g (8 oz) soft dark brown sugar

300 ml ($\frac{1}{2}$ pint) malt vinegar

1 Put the tomatoes, apples, onion and dates in a 2.75 litre ($4\frac{1}{2}$–5 pint) bowl. Cover with cling film, pulling back one corner to allow steam to escape and cook for 10 minutes. Stir halfway through cooking.

2 Stir in the ginger, cloves, spice, garlic, sugar and vinegar. Cook, uncovered, for 25 minutes or until thick. Stir after 10 minutes and 15 minutes. The correct consistency is reached when a wooden spoon drawn across the base of the bowl leaves a definite line.

3 While still hot, pour the chutney into three 450 g (1 lb) warm sterilised jars. Cover immediately with airtight and vinegar-proof tops. Label and leave to cool.

ORANGE CHUTNEY

MAKES ▶	ABOUT 1.4 kg (3 lb)
SETTING ▶	HIGH
TIME ▶	ABOUT 65 MINUTES
GRADING ▶	EASY

700 g (1½ lb) thin skinned oranges, pared, peeled, seeded and chopped

350 g (12 oz) onions, skinned and chopped

350 g (12 oz) cooking apples, peeled and chopped

225 g (8 oz) sultanas

450 ml (¾ pint) white wine vinegar

2.5 ml (½ level tsp) ground ginger

2.5 ml (½ level tsp) salt

5 ml (1 level tsp) ground mixed spice

1.25 ml (¼ level tsp) grated nutmeg

225 g (8 oz) soft dark brown sugar

1 Put the orange rind, orange flesh, onions and apples in a 2.75 litre (4½–5 pint) bowl. Cover with cling film, pulling back one corner to allow steam to escape and cook for 10 minutes.

2 Stir in the sultanas, vinegar, ginger, salt, spice, nutmeg and sugar. Cook, uncovered, for 55 minutes or until thick. Stir several times during cooking. The correct consistency is reached when a wooden spoon drawn across the base of the bowl leaves a definite line.

3 Spoon into three 450 g (1 lb) warm sterilised jars. Cover immediately with airtight and vinegar-proof tops. Label and leave to cool.

BANANA CHUTNEY

MAKES ▶	ABOUT 2.3 kg (5 lb)
SETTING ▶	HIGH
TIME ▶	ABOUT 28 MINUTES
GRADING ▶	EASY

450 g (1 lb) onions, skinned and chopped

6 bananas, peeled and chopped

225 ml (8 fl oz) malt vinegar

5 ml (1 level tsp) salt

5 ml (1 level tsp) curry powder

5 ml (1 level tsp) powdered ginger

100 g (4 oz) granulated sugar

275 g (10 oz) stoned dates, chopped

100 g (4 oz) sultanas

100 g (4 oz) currants

1 Put the onions in a 2.75 litre (4½–5 pint) bowl. Cover with cling film, pulling back one corner to allow steam to escape and cook for 8 minutes. Stir halfway through cooking.

2 Purée the bananas and vinegar in a blender or food processor. Stir the purée into the onions with the salt, curry powder, ginger, sugar, dates, sultanas and currants. Cover with cling film, pulling back one corner to allow steam to escape and cook for 10 minutes. Stir halfway through cooking.

3 Remove the cling film and continue to cook for 5 minutes. Stir in 150 ml (¼ pint) water and cook for a further 5 minutes until thick.

4 Spoon the chutney into five 450 g (1 lb) warm sterilised jars. Cover immediately with airtight and vinegar-proof tops. Label and leave to cool.

PICKLED ONIONS

MAKES ▶ 800 g (1¾ lb)
SETTING ▶ HIGH
TIME ▶ 4½ MINUTES
GRADING ▶ VERY EASY

50 g (2 oz) salt

700 g (1½ lb) pickling onions, skinned

600 ml (1 pint) malt vinegar

8 cloves

2.5 ml (½ tsp) whole allspice

8 black peppercorns

1 cm (½ inch) piece of cinnamon stick

1 small piece of ginger, bruised

1 In a large bowl, dissolve the salt in 300 ml (½ pint) water. Add over the onions and leave to soak for 24 hours.

2 Put the vinegar and spices in a 2 litre (3½ pint) bowl. Cover with cling film, pulling back one corner to allow steam to escape and cook for 4½ minutes or until boiling. Strain and cool.

3 Drain the onions and pack into jars. Pour the spiced vinegar over the onions. Cover with airtight and vinegar-proof tops and label. Leave for 1–2 months before use.

PICKLED RED CABBAGE

MAKES ▶ ABOUT 900 g (2 lb)
SETTING ▶ HIGH
TIME ▶ 12 MINUTES
GRADING ▶ VERY EASY

450 g (1 lb) red cabbage (after stalk removed), sliced

30 ml (2 level tbsp) salt

600 ml (1 pint) malt vinegar

7.5 g (¼ oz) cinnamon sticks

7.5 g (¼ oz) whole allspice

7.5 g (¼ oz) black peppercorns

6 cloves

1 Put the cabbage in a large bowl and sprinkle it with salt. Leave for 24 hours.

2 Drain the cabbage and pat dry with absorbent kitchen paper. Fill 2 jars with the cabbage.

3 Put all the remaining ingredients into a 1 litre (1¾ pint) jug. Cover with cling film, pulling back one corner to allow steam to escape and cook for 5 minutes or until boiling. Continue to boil for a further 7 minutes. Strain and set aside until cold.

4 Pour the cold vinegar over the cabbage. Cover with airtight and vinegar-proof tops and label.

CONFECTIONERY

MICROWAVE COURSE GUIDANCE NOTES

Always use a very large container when making confectionery with a high sugar content. For example, at least 2.75 litres ($4\frac{1}{2}$–5 pints).

Use a container made of a material which can withstand the high temperatures of boiling sugar and/or syrup. A large ovenproof glass bowl is ideal because you can see what is happening.

Never cover the container unless instructions are given to the contrary.

Use an oven cloth when handling the container as it gets very hot.

Never leave a conventional cooking thermometer in the container during cooking.

With sugar- and syrup-based confectionery make only the quantity given in the recipe and no more.

Do not leave the confectionery unattended while it is in the microwave cooker.

Watch chocolate carefully because if left too long in the microwave it will scorch. Cooking chocolate melts more quickly than dessert chocolate.

CHOCOLATE
COCONUT BALLS

MAKES ▶	8
SETTING ▶	HIGH
TIME ▶	2 MINUTES
GRADING ▶	VERY EASY

150 g (5 oz) plain chocolate, broken into pieces

1 egg yolk, size 2

15 g ($\frac{1}{2}$ oz) butter or margarine

2.5 ml ($\frac{1}{2}$ tsp) coffee essence

45 ml (3 level tbsp) desiccated coconut

1 Put the chocolate in a 1.2 litre (2 pint) bowl. Cook, uncovered, for 2 minutes or until melted. Stir frequently after 1 minute.

2 Beat in the egg yolk, butter and coffee essence. Set aside for about 30 minutes until the mixture becomes firm.

3 Using the palms of the hands, roll the mixture into balls the size of walnuts. Roll each ball in the desiccated coconut to coat completely.

4 Refrigerate until firm and place each in a sweet paper case.

——— TIP ———
IF PREFERRED, COAT IN FINELY CHOPPED NUTS.

WHITE DATES

MAKES ▶	ABOUT 45
SETTING ▶	HIGH
TIME ▶	$3\frac{1}{4}$ MINUTES
GRADING ▶	EASY

225 g (8 oz) stoned dates

65 g ($2\frac{1}{2}$ oz) marzipan

200 g (7 oz) white chocolate, broken into pieces

1 Fill the cavity of each date with a small piece of marzipan.

2 Put the chocolate into a 1.2 litre (2 pint) bowl. Cook, uncovered, for $3\frac{1}{4}$ minutes or until melted. Stir frequently after 1 minute.

3 Using 2 forks, dip and coat each date in chocolate. Place each on a piece of greaseproof paper.

4 Leave for 1–$1\frac{1}{2}$ hours until the chocolate has set. Put in small individual paper cases.

ORANGE **C**OFFEE **F**UDGE

MAKES ▶	ABOUT 14 PIECES
SETTING ▶	DEFROST and HIGH
TIME ▶	12½ MINUTES
GRADING ▶	LESS EASY

225 g (8 oz) granulated sugar

60 ml (4 tbsp) condensed milk

15 ml (1 tbsp) golden syrup

7.5 ml (1½ tsp) coffee essence

25 ml (1½ tbsp) orange juice

grated rind of 1 small orange

1 Put all the ingredients in a 2.75 litre (4½–5 pint) bowl. Cook, uncovered, on Defrost for 6½ minutes. Stir after 2, 4 and 6½ minutes.

2 Increase power setting to High. Continue cooking, uncovered, for 6 minutes or until 114°C (238°F) is reached on a sugar thermometer. Stir halfway through cooking.

3 Beat with an electric mixer until thick. Pour into a greased 15 cm (6 inch) tin. Leave for 30 minutes. Mark into squares, then leave until cold.

4 Break the fudge into pieces and put in individual paper cases.

SOFT **T**OFFEES

MAKES ▶	ABOUT 20
SETTING ▶	HIGH
TIME ▶	7 MINUTES
GRADING ▶	LESS EASY

40 g (1½ oz) butter or margarine

65 g (2½ oz) granulated sugar

22.5 ml (1½ tbsp) golden syrup

200 ml (7 fl oz) condensed milk

20 walnut halves, to decorate

1 Put the butter, sugar and syrup into a 2.75 litre (4½–5 pint) bowl. Cook, uncovered, for 2 minutes until sugar has dissolved. Stir halfway through cooking.

2 Stir in the condensed milk. Cook, uncovered, for 5 minutes or until 5 ml (1 tsp) of mixture forms a soft ball when dropped into a cup of cold water. Stir every 2 minutes.

3 Beat the mixture until the bubbles subside and the mixture is thick. Pour into a greased 15 cm (6 inch) tin. Set aside until cold enough to handle.

4 From the mixture into about 20 small balls. Place on greaseproof paper and press a walnut half on top of each.

5 Wrap in individual squares of greaseproof or sweet papers. Chill for several hours before serving. Store in the refrigerator.

INDEX